WHAT SHOULD CHRISTIANS DO?

WHEN THE
MOSQUE
COMES TO
TOWN

PASTOR KEVIN
(509) 697-7833

GINA WILSON

CHICK
PUBLICATIONS
Ontario, Calif 91761

For a complete list of distributors near you, call us at (909) 987-0771, or visit us online at: **www.chick.com**

Copyright © 2013 Gina Wilson

Published by:
CHICK PUBLICATIONS
P. O. Box 3500, Ontario, Calif. 91761-1019 USA
Tel: (909) 987-0771
Fax: (909) 941-8128
Web: www.chick.com
Email: postmaster@chick.com

Printed in the United States of America

ISBN: 978-0-7589-0966-4

Preface

While hundreds of books about Islam are available, few attempt to propose a biblical solution to the problem faced by communities that suddenly discover a mosque in their midst. Bible believers know that hearts must be changed before any significant cultural changes will occur. The focus of this book is to reach the hearts of individual Muslims.

The story goes that, 50 years ago, Muslim leaders in Islamic countries discouraged their people from moving to America because they feared they would be converted to Christ. The soul winning zeal of those days has dissipated in this country and we now have millions of Muslims living among us. Fear of each other has replaced the compassion that should be felt by Christians to weep for these lost souls bound by rituals that date back to the 7th century.

Gina Wilson's burden for Muslims began early on in life. After obtaining a bachelor's degree and completing several short-term missions trips, she received an appointment to work in a major Muslim country. This put her in direct contact with Muslim families and coworkers on a daily basis.

She came to understand that the commonalities of

life that bind all humans together are just as prevalent in Muslim societies. Through prayer and daily living out her relationship with Jesus, she found many opportunities to share the gospel. A pattern began to emerge in her witnessing that took into consideration the complexities of their culture and the open doors they provide. She has walked through those doors to effectively supply Muslims with information about the Jesus that they so misunderstand.

This book details some of the ways that Muslims will respond to a gentle, loving approach to sharing the gospel. Rather than view the Muslim neighbors in your community with fear or simply resign yourself to their presence, Wilson's experience and insight will give you a confident approach to drawing them out into friendship and showing them the true face of our loving Lord.

Note: In order to protect the author's identity and opportunities to speak freely to the Muslims around her, a pen name has been used. All names have been changed to protect the identities of the individuals included in this book.

Contents

Introduction

Muslims Move In

Whether Muslims move into the house next to you, a few blocks over, or begin gathering at their newly built mosque, a structure which resembles something you recognize from Aladdin and the 40 Thieves, the question has undoubtedly gone through your mind: What now?

What should you do when the mosque comes to town?

First and foremost, **do not run away, despair, or throw up your hands in defeat!**

There is a common reaction among the human race when approached by something unfamiliar and it sees people shying away from the unknown rather than approaching it. One thing I can tell you from personal experience is that the unknown is often scarier in our imagination than it is in reality.

In our imagination, Muslims are people completely unlike us who follow a religion we need to know thoroughly in order to reach for Christ. They are scary, unknown, and cannot possibly have anything in common with you or me.

In **reality** Muslims are people very much like you and me with the same concerns, fears, failures, hopes, desires and dreams. Parents want their children to get good grades, kids want their schoolmates to like them, girls dream of falling in love, and boys dream of owning their first car. As one who has lived among Muslims of all shades of religious fervor, I can tell you from personal experience, they are **very much** like you and me.

So... *what should you do when the mosque comes to town?*

Put on a smile.

Walk around the corner.

And say hello.

Yes, it really can be as simple as that.

Chapter 1

Saying Hello

You have new neighbors; you got up your courage and walked on over. Now what?

There are undoubtedly many thoughts going through your mind as you get ready to push that little button that will alert the whole household to your presence. Thoughts like: *I know that there are taboos in their culture! What are they? I don't want to offend them before I even get started! What if I accidentally offend them anyway?*

Let's take these questions one at a time.

Taboos

First: Men stick with men and women stick with women.

One of the easiest ways to show respect (and conversely offend your Muslim neighbors) is when dealing with members of the opposite sex. But don't worry! It's easy.

If you're a man: When first introducing yourself to your neighbor, if a woman comes to the door, ask for her husband. Do not introduce yourself or explain why you are there, just simply ask to see her husband. This seems rather rude in our western culture mindset, but to those from the Middle East, you are simply showing respect.

The husband or another male relative will show up and THEN you can paste on a big smile and say, "Hello! Welcome to the neighborhood!" If you want to make your new neighbor feel really special you could say, "Salaam-Alaykum!" Don't worry about getting the pronunciation right —they'll just love that you put forth the effort! The man will either invite you in or will come outside to chat with you. Muslims are very hospitable people and will not typically leave you standing awkwardly on the porch while they hide on the other side of the door.

If invited inside, do not fraternize with any women. They will probably make themselves rather scarce, but in case of their presence, always keep your attention directed to the male who you are speaking with. Even if she comes into the room to give you tea, direct your thanks of hospitality to the man.

If you're a woman: When first introducing yourself to your neighbor, if a man comes to the door, ask for his wife. You can state simply who you are ("I'm Dr. Jones' wife from down the street") but that is all. Striking up a conversation with a man is not seen as appropriate. If the woman you have come to see is not there, tell him simply you will come back another time. Do not go inside even if told that she will be back soon. Even if nothing untoward occurs, the male members of the family will see your behavior as loose.

It is possible that another woman will be called to come to the door. If this happens, feel free to smile and speak freely **to the woman**. The husband, brother, or male figure will probably stay at the door to see what you want, but do not address your greetings to him, just to the female member of his family.

If invited inside, latch onto the woman who has invited you. She may leave you alone for a brief time in order to make tea or bring some other refreshment, but she will come back quickly. Men will probably not speak with you and you should not try to speak with them. Some may sit in on the conversation you have with the female member of the family. Don't be intimidated! They're just curious and, since they can't talk with you directly, will sit and listen in on your conversation. Many a man has learned about Christ this way!

Second: No pig and no alcohol.

Women, this is especially important for you if you bring goodies over to welcome your new neighbors. When baking, the easiest thing to do is leave out the vanilla. Vanilla extract has alcohol and Muslims will not be able to eat it. Leave out the vanilla of any baked goods and you're good to go! Make your neighbor extra at-ease by cutting out a home-made tag with the label of your goodies and put the word 'Halal' on it. They will understand: No alcohol.

Men, this is especially important for you if you invite your Muslim guy friends over for a barbeque. As great and all-American as hotdogs are, many of those questionable links are made out of pork of some kind. BAN pork from a get-together where you are going to have your Muslim friends over. No pork = no problems.

Men and women both, keep this in mind whenever having Muslims over to your house. Never serve them an alcoholic drink or food with pork or pork products in it. Be especially careful with: hot dogs, canned spaghetti sauce, and vanilla extract.

Third and Final: You come from WHERE??

The last big item to be careful of is insulting where they come from. This may sound obvious, but this mistake is committed easier than you think. To our western minds, we see a corrupt regime and think, "What a horrible place! I pity the soul who comes from there!" It may just be, however, that your new neighbors hail from that location.

In general, Muslims are very loyal people. Instead of

speaking of the poor conditions of their country, they will most likely speak of their country's beauty, the traditions they remember from childhood, and other fond memories attached to the land. Some may bring up the corruption or poor conditions, but let them do the talking first and tread lightly. They may just want to vent; they're probably not looking for your "pro-American, high-minded" opinion.

If your neighbor comes from a country in which we have troops, they will not be happy about it. If the topic comes up, they will candidly express their decidedly negative opinion of our "meddling," but don't take it personally. Many Muslims have a two-fold problem: they do not like America in ideology but they love the benefits of living in the Land of Opportunity. While trying to remain loyal to their roots and ancestry, they will work through a paradigm shift during which, at some point, they will realize that they have ultimately become part of the America they "hate."

Keep in mind that your neighbor is interested in getting to know YOU, not the American government. Feel free to state your opinion when it is solicited — be yourself. They will still be getting to know YOU and will like YOU regardless of whether you agree or disagree about whether troops should march through the streets of Baghdad. Try to keep political talk to a minimum.

That's it! See? Wasn't that easy?

Now... what if you offend them anyway?

Each taboo above can be dealt with differently. If you accidentally find yourself falling into more conversation than appropriate with the wrong member of the human population, simply excuse yourself and seek out the correct gender. When the appropriate gender is found, or conversation is redirected to that person, remark how the other person you were talking to reminds you of your **brother** or **sister**, if you have the appropriate sibling.

If you lack the correct sibling, then you can simply say that the person you were talking to is just like the brother or sister you always wanted. By stating that you view them as a brother or sister you do two things:

1. You let them know you feel like they can be part of your family, and

2. You let them know you have no wrong motives whatsoever.

Using family language will be a very culturally appropriate way of saying, "I like you and your family and I feel comfortable around them."

If you accidentally bake with vanilla or serve up pork hotdogs at your backyard BBQ, apologize profusely and scramble to find something appropriate which they can eat. They know that all Americans "eat pork and drink beer" but even so, you do not want to substantiate the rather false view of all red, white, and blue blooded citizens. The best way to get out of a scrape of this kind is to simply plan ahead and avoid the awkward situation altogether.

Finally, should you find yourself in the rather uncomfortable position of having just insulted your new neighbor or friend's home country, apologize. Then be honest. Explain that you have always viewed it "this way" and that you have never heard good things about it. Apologize for your ignorance and invite them to tell you about all the good things about their country. Ask them to tell you where they would take you if you ever visited for a day. Ask about their favorite memories as a child or their favorite places to go. Ask them what they love about it. Your friend will be quick to forgive your ignorance and will regale you with a wealth of information that will reveal to you more about their heartbeat than you could possibly imagine.

Above all, be yourself. This is the most important part of beginning any relationship. We will all stumble over ourselves and botch attempts at crossing the cultural bridge. Be ready to laugh at yourself, apologize, learn from your mistakes, and try again. The more you interact with your neighbor, the more they will see your heart and sincere desire to know them as a person.

A sincere and genuine offer of friendship will speak far louder than any accidentally served pork sausages and flub-ups about their decrepit country. If you are willing to learn from your mistakes and correct them, your Muslim neighbor soon-to-be-friend will laugh right along with you. In time, you may even have some rather humorous stories to regale other friends with, that will have both you and your Muslim friend laughing through tears.

Chapter 2

Getting into Conversation

Once you have started getting to know your new Muslim friend or neighbor, there will undoubtedly be a time when you wonder about bringing God into your conversation. A question like the following might be very close to what you are thinking:

Based on their culture, how much do I need to get to know them before I bring up our difference in religion? Should I drop the idea altogether if they seem distant or plow ahead if they warmly respond to my overtures of friendship?

All great questions! One of the best aspects about reaching your Muslim friend for Christ is the fact that religious differences will be blatantly obvious and could potentially be spoken about right from the beginning. In general, a Muslim will assume that anyone who is not Muslim is a Christian. This is a beautiful thing! Because it means right off, before they even heard your western-accented "Salaam

Alaykum," they **knew** you were different. And they invited you in, anyway!

Muslims do not shy away from religious differences, nor do they shy away from religious discussion. To Muslims, God is a way of life: a way of speaking, eating, breathing, working, playing, and think- ing. God is to be brought into every conversation, thought, and action. As with any "rule," there will be exceptions, but in general, Muslims will at least mention God in nearly every conversation (if only to say "In sha'Allah" —"God-willing"). Here is where we western Christians need to learn something. God should be **our** way of life, too! Jesus Christ should be in every thought, breath, and action of our own. If He is, conversation about Him will flow as naturally as asking your neighbor what the baseball scores were from last night's game.

Live, breathe, and act Jesus Christ. As you are first getting to know your neighbor, do not make your "religion" a secret! Be absolutely 100% open about who you are. If they ask about your weekend activi- ties, tell them you go to church to worship God. If you are speaking about hobbies and you read the Bible daily, talk about it. If something in your conver- sation reminds you of a Bible verse you read, share that with them. Do not be afraid to make Jesus front and center in your conversations. When you do, your neighbor will realize that you're serious about the God you worship.

Let me give you a GREAT BIG WARNING. If you do NOT share anything about your identity in Christ at the first available opportunity, your neighbor will think you don't worship God at all. God is the first thing on their tongues. So He should be on ours. By genuinely speaking of Jesus, Muslims will be brought into conversation and desire to know this One of whom you speak so fondly. If you leave the subject until later, they will wonder why you haven't spoken about it previously, calling into question the sincerity of your faith.

Westerners have become very assimilated to the cultural way of thinking about religion: it's okay to speak of in church, with your church group, or in a small group in Starbucks. But don't say anything too loudly because you might offend a stranger. Don't believe me? Ever heard of the phrase, "God and politics?" It's usually used in conjunction with "Don't speak about...," not "Let the whole world hear!" If you love Jesus, show it! Speak about Him, breathe Him, love Him through your actions.

One of the most important ways you can love Jesus through your actions is in simply getting to know the Muslim down the street. What do I mean? Namely this: Get to know the soul you desire to see saved before you preach at it. Muslims will typically welcome a genuine offer of friendship. They will appreciate your fumbling attempts at learning their language. They will enjoy your baked goods and warmly offer their hospitality. But they are doing this for a friend –someone they are getting to know, someone who has demonstrated love and a caring attitude —not someone who only wants to step inside their house, tell them to change, and leave.

If you desire to reach these least-reached people, be committed. Like any relationship, it will need to be cultivated. You will benefit from them and they from you. The eastern culture is one of warmth, sharing, and closeness. When you pass from stranger to friend, in their eyes, you might as well be part of the family.

This means that they might call on you to help out if they are in a jam, will possibly invite you to take part in wedding preparations and celebrations, and will be more than happy if you stay at their house 'till all hours of the night drinking tea and chatting. This does not mean that you have to make them your "best friends" but it does mean that your offer of friendship needs to be real.

Christ in Conversation

So after you've visited with Fatima several times, learned the names of her three children who are all grown and in college, and know that she wishes for nothing more than to see her mother come from Iraq, how do you begin talking about Jesus or the Bible?

Through prayer!

You may be thinking, *I asked you how to TALK to them, not pray for them,* but stay with me and I will show you exactly why prayer must begin every profitable conversation you will have with a Muslim.

For our purposes, prayer does three main things. Firstly, it removes you from the picture. When you focus on the One who needs to work in your friend's heart, you will come to the point of realizing that you cannot say nor do anything that will make your friend believe. You are simply an agent who is willing to be used of the Lord in this person's life.

Secondly, it causes you to give all glory to God. The more you realize that you cannot do anything and that God is the one who must work, when conversations arise and parts of the gospel are shared, glory will be given to the One who brought that conversation to pass.

Finally, prayer keeps you close to God. You've undoubtedly heard it before, but prayer is conversation with God: your spirit with His. He uses it to draw you near to His heart, make His desires yours, give you wisdom, increase your faith, and cultivate the loving, tender relationship of which you desire to testify.

In Ephesians 6, Paul wraps up his address to the Christians at Ephesus by highlighting several very important aspects of the Christian life. He writes about the armor of God in v.10-17, then concludes the section with these words in v. 18-19, exhorting them to be, "Praying always with all prayer and supplication in the Spirit, and watching thereunto with all perseverance and supplication for all saints; **And for me, that utterance may be given unto me, that I may open my mouth boldly, to make known the mystery of the gospel..."** (Ephesians 6:18-19).

The emphasis is obviously mine, but I want to make the point. Look what he asks them to be praying for —utterance! Conversation! To what end? "To make known the mystery of the gospel!" During his lifetime, Paul was used of the Lord to reach many gentile nations who had never heard the name of Jesus Christ. Through his ministry thousands of people were gathered into the folds of Christ's kingdom. He would be what many consider a "professional evangelist" and what did he ask for? Prayer for conversations!

Prayer is by far the most crucial aspect to beginning a gospel-oriented conversation with your Muslim friend. If you try to draw your Muslim friend into conversation about spiritual things without prayer, it will never work. Every attempt will leave you grasping at straws. Make your new friendship and desire for gospel-conversations a daily point of prayer. Pray about it in the morning, pray about it at night. Keep it ever close to your heart. When prayer is involved the rewards will be astounding!

Questions Asked of You

Questions are amazing things! When questions are asked of you by your Muslim friend a few things happen:

- You have free reign to answer them openly, honestly, and thoroughly.

- They are generally more open to you because they are leading the conversation regarding spiritual matters.

- The Lord has just revealed what topic to cover!

The Lord works in mysterious ways in the hearts of Muslims. He draws them through dreams, hopes and desires, disillusionment with Islam, and life circumstances. When your Muslim friend asks a spiritual question, they are usually speaking directly out of the Lord's working in their hearts. They will ask the questions most pressing to them. All you have to do is answer!

Keep in mind: If a Muslim asks you a spiritual question they are saying that they trust you. It can take months before a Muslim will get up the courage to ask you anything about the way you worship. Approaching serious discussion about Christianity in the form of sincere desire can be dangerous for Muslims (yes, even those living in the good ol' U. S. of A.). So bear this in mind when a sincere question is asked of you. What is asked of you in confidence, you would be wise not to share with the rest of his or her Muslim family.

Questions Asked by You

Asking questions of your Muslim friends about their religion is another good way to bring them into conversation about the gospel. When you ask honest questions of your friend it does several things. First, it tells them that you honestly want to know about them and their way of life. This will help them see that you are a friend who is thoroughly interested in them.

Secondly, more than any book will be able to do, you will learn where your Muslim friend stands on issues of religion that you may have only heard rumors about. Finally, you will begin to see how you can take their understanding of religion and life and use it as a bridge to explaining the glorious truths of the gospel.

The Truth about Speaking

There will be many and diverse opportunities to share the gospel! A question about church, an accusation about the Bible, and curiosity about why you love Jesus can all lead to gospel conversations. They can happen when you sit down for tea, go shopping, or are enjoying a backyard BBQ. This is another reason why prayer is so crucial. Gospel conversations do not happen according to a schedule. They occur because the Holy Spirit draws the unbeliever to Himself and you need to be prepared "to give an answer to every man that asketh you a reason of the hope that is in you…" (1 Peter 3:15).

Be Prepared

I know what you're thinking: **Oh no, here it comes —the dreaded homework!** You're probably envision-ing hours upon hours of reading through books big enough to make you remember college days. After all don't you need to know everything about Islam and Muslims in order to "be prepared?"

No! I am not going to ask you to read the Qur'an or memorize the Hadith (or even find out what the Hadith are). Your Muslim friend will take care of making sure you know the ins and outs of Islam. I **am** asking you to read your Bible.

There is a reason why preparation was stressed in Peter's first epistle. Let's walk through the following scenario and I believe you will understand why I, with Peter, am stressing this point.

You have gotten to know Abdulla for a while now and have been faithfully praying for an opportunity to share the gospel with him.

One day as you are barbequing hamburgers in your back yard, he turns to you and says, "John, I have watched you and your wife. I know there is something different about you. You are not like the Christians my father always told me about. I want to ask something of you."

You flip a burger, excitedly send heavenward a two-second prayer for help and say, "Anything my friend! Ask away."

Abdulla gathers his courage and asks. "Why do you believe Jesus is God?"

This is no Sunday school question, you think to yourself. **Here it goes!**

"Well in the first four books of the New Testament where Jesus' life is recorded He says that He and the Father are one. The Father is God. So when Jesus says that He is one with the Father, He is essentially saying He and God are the same."

Abdulla takes a drink of his soda. "You believe that the Father is God. Jesus says He is one with the Father so He is saying He is the same as God."

"Yep! That's right," you affirm. "Jesus made Himself equal with the Father."

Abdulla considers what you have said then asks, "Where in the Bible does it say that?"

"I can't remember chapter and verse," you amicably reply, "but I can look it up later for you, if you'd like."

"You do not know where it can be found?" Abdulla challenges. "You do not read your Bible?"

You vigorously nod your head. "Yes, I do! Every day! I just cannot remember the exact part. I'll look it up for you when we go inside."

Abdulla considers this, then levels his last accusation that ends a now rather awkward conversation.

"You believe God had a son with a woman? That is blasphemy! God is a spirit! He does not have relations with women! How can you say such a thing?"

You stand there slack jawed as a burger turns into charcoal. What on earth do you say to that? You wrack your brain for another explanation of Jesus' Godhead and come up empty.

Now, you might be thinking, ***I'm sure that's an extreme case*** but let me assure you —it is most definitely not! Muslims **will** question where things are written in the Bible and **will** question what you mean by what you say. In the course of this book, I will give you some "quick tips" on how to approach questions such as the "Sonship" of Christ and His deity, as well as those Bible verses you have yet to memorize. For now, I will simply let the illustration stand to admonish you —be prepared!

Chapter 3

Real Conversations

Now that you've got a fairly good handle on some of the ins and outs of conversing with Muslims, I want to give you a practical look at some real life conversations. The following conversations did occur and though names have been changed, the circumstances and dialogue are factual. Each conversation will highlight a different aspect of bringing the gospel into your everyday dialogue with Muslim friends.

Conversation 1
Serving God

Miriam and I had gotten to know each other, off and on, over the course of several months. She knew I was a Christian and was quite comfortable and open around me. One day as we were speaking about our families, Miriam asked me, "Don't you miss them?"

"I do!" I replied. "My family and I are all very close."

"So why do you live here away from them?"

"Because God wants me here." I went on to explain just what I meant. "My life is not my own, I live for the Lord. He made the way for each of us to know Him and have a relationship with Him. I love Him; He's everything to me. The least I can do is go where He wants me. This may not be my favorite place, but I am 100% positive that the Lord has me here for a reason. He's given me a love for the people here and opportunities to get to know them. He has taught me a lot about who He is, too. God's grown me in understanding Him in a way I never would have, otherwise."

Miriam looked a bit misty-eyed as she replied, "That is a wonderful way to live."

She proceeded to tell me about a time when she and her family were in a place she absolutely hated. She said she cried every night and asked Allah why she had to be there. In the end, she stated, she knew it was God's will. But there was no love or depth of relationship for God borne out of her circumstances.

Miriam had to leave after our brief exchange but even though it was quite short, she was given a glimpse into what it looks like to live for and serve a God who cares.

Conversation 2
Modesty and the Gospel

Sometimes the best conversations happen during

the shortest amount of time or in the places least expected. This is certainly the case with a conversation between Aisha and myself.

I did not know Aisha very well and had not been given a chance to speak with her. One day, on our way into the movie theater with some friends, Aisha turned to me and said, "Are you religious? I notice that you always dress well (modestly), not like the other westerners here. Are you religious? I know there are Catholics and Pentecostal. Are you one of those?"

"I worship and serve Jesus Christ," I stated. "His name is Isa in the Qur'an and I worship Him as God, as Isa al Masih (Jesus the Messiah)."

"Oh, you are a Massihi!" she exclaimed, understanding that I am a Christian who worships Jesus.

"Yes," I affirmed. "I read the Bible, God's Holy Word, and live for Him. Jesus states that we are to dress in such a way that people will see Him in us, rather than what we look like on the outside. I love Him and dressing modestly is one way I can obey and serve Him."

"That is very good," she thoughtfully whispered as we walked into the darkened theater.

Little did I know the impact of this simple conversation. Four months later, she began to open up and ask me questions about life as a Christian and the validity of the Bible. Sometimes, the smallest conversations can have the biggest impact.

Conversation 3
God is God of All People

The God of the Bible is God over all people! This exclamation and positive affirmation is the main point of the next conversation. To Muslims, god speaks Arabic, wants prayers in Arabic, expects devotion in Arabic, and worship via the holy Qur'an in Arabic. When Muslims think of the "western God" they are often of the erroneous opinion that He is only the God of English-speaking people. I love bringing up God's omni-qualities in conversation to show Muslims that God is much, much more than they ever considered Him to be.

One such opportunity occurred during a "team building" exercise with my fellow employees. We had been assigned to bring an item that represented our lives to show the group. I decided to make this a witnessing opportunity and brought my Bible.

During the team building exercise, I was placed at a table with a lady from Kenya, another from South Africa, and a local Arab. The Kenyan went first and much to my surprise and delight, she brought out her Bible. It was written in her native tongue and she went on to explain why it was of such importance to her and how the God of the Bible had changed her life. My Arab coworker was fascinated.

The South African went next and again, much to my delight, pulled out her Afrikaans Bible. She, too, explained why the Bible was so important to her and how she served the God of the Bible with her life.

Finally, I went, briefly reiterating my own devotion to and love for the Bible and the God who is revealed through it. I went on to explain to my Arab coworker just what she was seeing. We all had the same Bible in our own languages because Jesus is God of **all** people —all tribes, all nations and tongues.

"Even Arabs?" she asked.

"Yes!" I excitedly affirmed. "Everyone! God works all over the world. He wants **all** people to worship Him. This is why He made His Holy Word available to be read in all languages."

"It's the same?" she asked.

"Yes!" I again affirmed. "It is the exact same Bible and we all worship the same God."

Three people from totally different areas of the planet, all with different family backgrounds and native tongues, all worshipping the One true God. The Lord used us that day to demonstrate a beautiful principle: the God of the Bible is the God of **all** people.

Our Arab coworker found herself quite speechless.

Conversation 4
Jesus Christ

It is not often that a conversation will be blatantly about Jesus Christ. More often than not, well placed questions or statements will lead the conversation there. But there are rare times when a searching soul will boldly bring up the topic that is typically considered taboo. Such conversations are a complete joy.

One day while I was going about my work, a friend of mine noticed a YouTube picture of a man praying. She stopped me before the picture changed with the music and asked, "What is that man doing?"

I looked at the picture and replied, "He's praying."

"What's that?" she replied in wide-eyed wonder.

"You know, talking with God," I stated.

"What?!" she said, aghast. "No man can talk with his God!"

"Sure you can." I replied with a smile that said I knew more than I was saying. "I do! Every day!"

"How do you talk with God? How can you know God? God doesn't know us. How can you talk with God?" My friend was all questions and more eager than I had ever known anybody to be in her desire to know more about this God whom I affirmed to be knowable.

Over the course of many days following, we sat down and discussed first and foremost how one can know God —namely through Jesus Christ. We spoke all about Jesus, elaborated on who He is as revealed through the Bible, and discussed many details related to His work in the world. Finally, we got down to the brass tacks of explaining that Jesus is God's way of providing for us a substitute to take our punishment and enter into relationship with Him.

During one of our last conversations before she left the country, she looked at me with rather sad eyes and said, "If I believe in this, my family would not like it."

"That is probably true," I agreed.

"They do not believe in this. They say it is not true."

"But what do you believe?" I gently questioned.

My friend was very quiet. She knew that Jesus knew her name, knew how many hairs were on her head, had a plan for her from the beginning of the world and loved her more than she could ever dream. But she also knew that if she committed to worship God through Jesus Christ, she could be in real trouble with her family. She sadly walked away, hope in her heart, fear in her eyes, and indecision warring in her soul.

Pray for her. She still has not decided to follow Him.

Conversation 5
The Bible is Corrupt!

Some conversations can appear to start off in a hostile way. When this happens, take heart! Your friend may not actually be hostile toward you, just toward something they were told. This is certainly the case for the following conversation I had with a coworker. I had not known this particular lady very long, but she knew I was a Christian and felt I was trustworthy enough to ask questions regarding my beliefs.

One day as we were waiting for a meeting to begin, she turned to me and asked, "When you go home, do you wear a bikini?"

I laughed, amused, and answered, "No, of course not. I follow what the Bible says no matter where I am. I dress the same way at home as I do here. God tells me through the Bible to dress modestly in a way that will please Him and I do."

She then launched her attack. "Why do you read the Bible? It has been corrupted."

Note: Many Muslims believe this, not because they have done any research, but simply because they have been told by their local imam that Christianity is a false religion and that the Bible has been changed over time.

"What part has been changed?" I challenged.

"I don't know exactly what part but it has been," she returned.

I confidently and excitedly told her, "Not one verse in the Bible has been changed. My Bible is the exact same document as the very first manuscripts ever found. The earliest manuscripts of the Bible, like the Dead Sea Scrolls, are the **exact** same as my Bible!"

"Really?" This was new information to her.

"Yes! We have the exact same Bible. Even Muhammad told his followers to read the Bible. Nothing has been changed."

"Well, my husband said it has been changed," she again countered.

"Ask him to show you what has been changed. I guarantee you he won't be able to find it."

She thought about what I had said and finally replied, "Maybe I will read the Bible and see."

The meeting was called to order shortly after this bold statement.

When conversing with Muslims, keep in mind that we serve a powerful, perfect, and mighty God. His has kept words safe through the centuries and they are perfect and true. Once a person begins to read His word, it will not return void!

Conversation 6
Jesus in Her Heart

One day as I was going about my regular work routine, a coworker pulled a friend of hers into my office. Excited, she turned to me and said, "Gina, Rachel is a Christian too! She says she's born again. Is that what you are?"

I nodded and gave a cautious "yes" not entirely sure what she meant by the phrase.

Without missing a beat, my coworker turned to her friend, Rachel, and said (of me), "I wasn't sure what she called herself but I knew she had Jesus in her heart."

I inwardly rejoiced for such a testimony. Often times Muslim friends will want to label Christians with a brand of Christianity they are familiar with, but in doing so they will miss the big picture. Here, this friend of mine wasn't sure what I "called myself" but knew Who I worshipped. She had gotten the big picture and for that I rejoiced.

Conversation 7
We Need to Pray!

Never discount your witness and testimony with kids. Sometimes the best conversations can happen with children.

One day I was watching several of my friends' children. We were having an enjoyable time together, but they eventually began to get restless. They were not allowed to go out of the house on this day, even with an adult, and were none too happy. As their rudeness toward me rose a level, the call to prayer sounded from a nearby mosque. All of the children began to shout out, "We need to go pray! We need to go pray!"

After reiterating the fact that their mothers had given strict instruction that they were to stay inside that day, I decided it was time for a little talk.

Note: I knew these particular children quite well and was a bit of a mother figure to them. A rebuke like the following was appropriate in this case. I don't know that I would recommend doing this during a first-time babysitting stint.

"Abdulla," I began sternly, addressing the oldest boy. "Do you think God would be more pleased by you saying a few memorized words instead of respecting and obeying the one He has put in authority over you?"

All of the boys gave that some thought but still maintained that they needed to go pray.

"What happens if you don't go pray?" I demanded.

"We have to!" they again affirmed.

"But what happens if you don't," I persisted.

"We'll go to hell" another boy finally admitted.

"But that's only when we're older," a third boy entered the conversation.

"So do you think you will be able to pray five times a day every day when you are older? Do you think you will be able to do that perfectly?" I asked, this time a bit gentler.

"No. Probably not," Abdulla admitted.

"So you can't be perfect, but if you aren't God will throw you into hell."

The boys quickly sobered to the discussion.

"Boys, no one is perfect. Before God no one, not even the best person you can think of, is good enough to stand before God because God is totally perfect. We all do bad things. We can never work hard enough or pray enough times to earn our way to God. Only God can take away the bad things we do and make the way for us to go to heaven to be with Him."

Each boy considered what I had said, thinking over their own bad things, knowing that they could never make up for all the times they had been rude to their parents, their teachers, and even myself that afternoon. They understood clearly the concept of sin and the need for some kind of punishment to clear that sin away.

Though their parents came before we were able to go any farther with our conversation that day, during days succeeding this, the boys were full of questions whenever I saw them. I was privileged to walk them through the entire Bible, starting with Genesis, showing them the plan God always had for a Saviour, one He would provide, that would take away the sin of the world. We talked about Jesus and His life on earth and what He did for us so that we could have a relationship with God.

Though the boys have not yet made any decisions, they show a hunger and desire to know Jesus. Their favorite story is that of the gospel and they ask me to retell it to them nearly every time I see them. One boy has expressed the fact that his family doesn't believe these things about Jesus and his concern over their reaction were he ever to worship Jesus.

I may never know if they decide to believe in and worship the One true God, but seeds have been planted. Some plant, others water, and God gives the increase. I pray the seeds that have been planted inside these boys will someday sprout and grow into a beautiful plant in the kingdom of God. Never discount conversations with children —you never know where they may lead.

Note: I know for a fact that these boys have

discussed what I told them with their families. This is only natural and gives me further reason to be excited —not only have these boys heard the gospel, but now their families have heard it through them as well. Do not be intimidated by this thought of conversation-sharing. As mentioned earlier, if you are a Christian, their parents would expect nothing less from you than to discuss your faith when it is asked about —even by their children.

The parents may ask that you refrain from talking about spiritual things with their children, in which case you should stop. If questions are still asked by their kids, store those questions away, and talk to their parents. Discuss the question and answer in case they would like to tell their children for you. In all likelihood, their children will never hear the answer to their question but their parents have just been given a bit of the gospel. And if those kids are anything like the many I have known throughout the years, they will be curious enough that they will not stop wanting to know.

Chapter 4

Real Situations

Now for some "real situations" Q and A. These are questions straight from "you" —people who have very little experience interacting with Muslims who desire to reach them for the gospel.

Q: *Is relationship witnessing the only way, or is there a way, in a chance meeting of five minutes, to give a Muslim something to cook on? If so, what would be a suitable topic and how to broach it?*

A: As with anyone, there is never one "right" way. Muslims respond to relationship witnessing the most, simply due to their culture. Culturally, if a man stands on the sidewalk and preaches, Americans will gather around and listen if for no other reason than pure amusement. Muslims will not typically do this. They listen to someone they trust.

However, if you run into a Muslim and want to give him something to think about in the few minutes you have at a grocery store or car parts place, hand them a tract. I make a habit of passing out tracts in American gas stations when I meet Muslim cashiers.

Typically, I make a note of their name and ask the man or woman where they are from, explaining that I have lived in the Middle East. I will briefly inquire as to whether they have any family in their home country or if they have all moved to America. After a brief conversation, I will pull out a tract and tell them that the booklet is a story about Muslims. I will invite them to read it and tell them that when I come back again I would like to know what they thought of it.

If I know I will not be through that particular gas station again, I will just simply say it is a gift for them and I hope they enjoy it. This method of giving a tract with an invitation to discuss its contents and "gifting" it to a friend or stranger works well, whether you will see the person once a week or once in a lifetime.

Tracts really are a great way to get the gospel into the hand of a Muslim when you have a very limited amount of time. I do say this with a warning ringing in my mind, however. Please be very careful concerning what type of tract you hand out. A fiery religious tract that sets out to point out all the evils with Islam probably wouldn't be the best way to go. Be sure that the tract, whether story form or booklet, sets about to share the hope and truth of the gospel. A vendetta against Islam is not what you are preaching. "Is Allah Like You" and "Your Best Life" (published by Chick Publications) are two excellent Muslim-specific tracts you can use. "A Love Story" and "Who Is He" (also from Chick Publications) are also excellent tracts which will help to share the gospel as clearly and concisely as possible.

Q: *If you are conversing and you get stumped by a question, what is the most gracious way to continue?*

A: Be honest. Tell them that their question is not one you have thought of before. But don't leave it there! Tell them that you will search the Bible to find the answer. They may be a bit put off by the fact that you don't know every verse and chapter, but you could do worse damage and turn them away forever if you do not follow up with their question and find the answer. Be sure to find the answer in a timely manner (within the week, so it will still be fresh in their mind) and then get back to them with it. Though they may not show it, they will be impressed that you cared enough to find the answer to their question. Your actions can then open further doors for conversations about the gospel.

Q: *If a conversation is wandering into subjects that are not going to lead to fruitful discussion, how do you graciously bring it back on track? What would be some of the fruitful topics and which would be a distraction?*

A: This can be a tricky one. It also depends on what one views as unfruitful. As with any relationship, there will be times of trouble and frustrations that might get voiced. Anger toward their home country, their host country, family troubles, children worries, hopes for greater fortune —you name it and conversations will run the gamut. I tend to go with the opinion that nothing short of gossip is unfruitful. Nearly any bit of discussion can lead to you pointing your Muslim friend toward the gospel. Though the possibilities are quite literally endless, let me take a stab at giving you just a few examples of how a bad, good, or otherwise conversation can still be used to point your friend toward the gospel.

My one tip before I continue is this: Whenever engaging in discussion (and this goes for conversations with anyone, really) always have your "feelers" up for ways you can link life to the gospel. You'll begin to see how this works out below. It takes practice, but once you get the hang of it, it will begin to feel as natural as breathing.

When conversations turn toward the negative when speaking of politics: When conversations turn toward the negative about a country or ruler, I try to direct conversation back to the One True King and Rulcr, the Creator of heaven and earth. I will bring up verses that speak about the nations and people in comparison with the greatness of God. (In chapter 8 I will include Bible passages that are helpful for conversations like these.) I will also discuss what the Bible says about the return of The King one day to rule in perfection. This is something you can speak about whenever the subject of politics comes up and the conversation tends toward frustration and complaint rather than constructive criticism.

When conversations seem to be all about wealth and how to amass more: I will typically bring up Jesus' words about the rich man entering into heaven. If possible I will even take out the Bible and read those verses straight from the Word. I will ask questions, steering the conversation toward what wealth is and whether riches here on earth can ever truly satisfy. This will probably lead to a "good-deeds" discussion —riches do not satisfy, but doing good things for less fortunate people does satisfy.

If the person is a self-proclaimed righteous or "good-enough" Muslim, I will take our conversation about riches one step further. Just as no amount of wealth will buy our way into heaven; neither will any amount of "good deeds" we do. No one can stand before a Holy and perfect God no matter how much we "do" because we are not perfect enough. Have them think of the best person they know and relate the fact that regardless of how good that person is, perfection can never be earned. This leaves us hopeless when it comes to standing before God. Right? Wrong! God provided a way by taking the punishment of our bad deeds on Himself!

When conversations about the gospel seem to be going nowhere or feel like one giant debate that no one will "win": Change the topic all together. If yours is any kind of true friendship, then, as with all friendships, patience needs to be had. Don't throw all of your relationship building away because your friend is in a huff about what you believe and is determined to make you lose the discussion. Remember, it could be that they are resisting the Spirit's pull and are arguing out of fear. They could also just have a very hard heart. If they rebuff you constantly and refuse to hear anything about what you believe, it might be wise to take a step back. Possibly even distance yourself from that relationship.

They began to be friends with you, knowing quite early on (I hope!) that you were a Christian. If they start to want to be friends with you but have nothing to do with your spirituality, that will be impossible (again, I hope!). Christ is to be what you eat, live, breathe, and think on a minute-by-minute basis. Your friend should not be able to go through one conversation with you without hearing something about the One you worship (even if all you say is a brief "Praise the Lord").

If they want nothing to do with that and forbid you from saying anything about the Lord, it would be wise to withdraw yourself from that relationship. This can be hard, but withdrawal serves a few purposes. One, it lets your friend know you are serious about your relationship with God. Two, it shows your friend what life is like in absence of you. That might sound strange, but your witness is more powerful than you think. You are likely the only source of Jesus in their lives; when that sweetness is pulled away, the absence will be noticed.

Third, it can be used to draw your friend back into relationship with you. Sometimes the old adage, "absence makes the heart grow fonder," can be quite apt when dealing with friendships. Instead of continuing to clash and argue, absence will cause both parties to reevaluate and when ready, come back into a friendship more willing to listen to each other and explain, rather than argue and debate.

When the person is adamantly opposed to hearing anything about the gospel: As hard as it is, this could be time to pull the plug. Don't stop praying and keep the offer for friendship open, but if they want nothing to do with God or hearing it from you, it might be time to take a step back for a long while. Your friend or neighbor will not stop watching you. You still live a daily witness before them through your actions. I have had Muslim friends I've not spoken with in ages come up and strike up a conversation as if we had never left off.

Christ is a powerful magnet; He is also a stumbling block. In the course of your friendship, you will likely witness both occurring in your friend's life, evidencing itself in a deepening friendship or a period of separation out of frustration, desire, or fear regarding what you have told them through the Gospel. Take heart: it is not you or I who draw Muslims to Jesus; it is Jesus, Himself. He will work in their hearts whether we have an active friendship or not. We are just the messengers as we are given opportunity to be so.

Fruitful vs. Unfruitful Topics of Discussion

Here I will list the top three areas to pursue in conversation as well as three you should avoid and the reasons why.

Fruitful Conversation Topics

1. God's love

To Muslims, god **can** love; to those of us who worship the living God, He **is** love. Muslims do not know a God who literally defines love, who planned the inception of the world through it and redeemed all of mankind by it. They have no understanding of "God IS love." Conversations in which you can relay to your Muslim friends that the God you serve is a loving God will have a powerful and profound impact. Make it clear that you love God —because He **first** loved you! Make it clear that God loves them too —yes, even now when they do not love Him back!

2. God's plan for their lives

Most Muslims view life with a rather fatalistic outlook. "If Allah wills it, then it will be so." The concept that God has a plan for their lives and desires to know them intimately will come as a pleasant surprise. This, along with the love God has for them, are two of the most "drawing" aspects of the gospel. Friends of mine have been very impacted by scriptures such as Psalm 139, wherein God states clearly that He KNOWS them —and knew them before they were even born! They also treasure verses like Matthew 10:29-30, "Are not two sparrows sold for a farthing? And one of them shall not fall on the ground without your Father. But the very hairs of your head are all numbered."

3. God's "knowability"

Now obviously we cannot perfectly know God —the Bible is clear on that (see I Corinthians 13:12). But we most certainly can, to a degree, know God, be intimately connected with Him, speak with Him, hear His voice, be lead of Him, loved by Him, and known of Him. This is something utterly foreign for Muslims. Though Muslims will tell you that Allah is "gracious and compassionate, full of mercy" they do not understand those things in the way we do.

What they are saying is that Allah is gracious when he wants to be, compassionate when he wants to be, and full of mercy when he wants to be. He is not always this way nor is he bound to always be so. When we say God is gracious, compassionate, and merciful we are saying that God IS grace, He IS compassion, and He IS mercy, just like He IS love. He defines those things and from Him we gain our definition and understanding of them. God is always perfectly loving, gracious, merciful, compassionate and will never turn away from being so "for in him there is no shadow of turning," (James 1:17).

Unfruitful Conversation Topics

1. Evils of Islam

The western world has made a few things quite blatantly clear to Muslims, one of those being that Islam
is evil. Now, I am aware that in recent years varying
political powers have made steps toward undoing
this perception, but regardless, the large majority
of the Arab world thinks Westerners hate them. As
such, if you begin a friendship with a Muslim, the last
thing you want to start bringing up is all that is evil or
wrong with Islam. Is Islam evil? Yes —just as much as
any false religion. But will saying so draw your Muslim
friends to ask questions about Christ? No. It will push
them away.

Use your imagination with me for a second and con-
jure up the following scene:

You have just moved to a new country and know
very few people. Your next door neighbors seem
nice enough even though they worship a different
god than you.

One day your neighbors come over and say, "Hello,
welcome to the neighborhood. We noticed you just
moved in and would like to invite you to dinner. Can
you come over tonight?"

Flattered, you say yes. Five o'clock comes around
and you find yourself at their front door. Your

neighbors welcome you in and you all sit down to dinner. You begin talking and find that you enjoy their company. They are quite upfront about their religion but you don't really mind. Then, right about in time for dessert they ask you about your religion. Heat creeps up your collar because you know they probably won't be quite appreciative but you tell them anyway. They listen and give solemn nods of acknowledgement. Dessert goes by without incident.

When you move into the living room to chat while enjoying after-dinner coffee, the host turns to you and says, "How can you worship a god like that? Your god tells you to dress strangely and kill people. Your religion is evil. Our religion is nothing like that. Have you ever considered it?"

You are quite taken aback, not understanding what these hosts are saying since you don't think your religion is "evil" and either, a) mutter some nearly in-coherent reply if you are shy or, b) feel like throttling them if that is the bent of your temper. What had been a rather pleasant evening turned into an upsetting one, making you wish you had moved to the other house across the city that was also an option. If nothing else, you will certainly never dine with these neighbors again!

That is what discussing all the "evils" of Islam can be like to Muslims. Many Muslims do not consider Islam evil (otherwise they would not be Muslims!), and would be quite offended to hear you say something to that degree. Rather than bringing up what is wrong with their religion, offer them a glimpse of the right and true relationship you have with the Living God.

2. Denigration of the Prophet Muhammad

This is a great big "no-no." All Muslims revere the Prophet Muhammad and usually add a "peace be upon him" whenever uttering his name. He is the absolute example of what a Muslim should be and the capstone of the Muslim faith. There really is no reason why he needs to be brought up in your conversations, and it is better that way. Muhammad has very little which is worthy of commenting on, so, in this case, "if you don't have something nice to say, don't say anything at all."

Muslims will defend Muhammad up one side and down the other, regarding everything he did as right and good —from marrying as many wives as he deemed worthy, to his slaughter of thousands as he raided Arabian lands. Simply stay away from this one and you won't have anything to worry about.

3. Personal Issues

This is similar to the "evils of Islam" topic. Personal vendettas against women wearing head scarves, the evils of covering women in black sheets, the lack of women's rights, or the amount of Muslim terrorists, who are moving into the west at an ever increasing rate, will not be helpful in the least if you are trying to draw your friend toward the gospel. Muslims have been looked down upon, denigrated, and out-right hated for years on end by the West. If they even get a whiff of accusation regarding who they are and the way they worship (seen as one and the same to them), they will immediately go on the defensive.

It is better to put your own personal issues on the backburner and let them stay there. I am not saying to stay silent regarding these issues if you can sincerely use them to reveal the beauty of the gospel (which is possible!). But if you have a chip on your shoulder about one aspect of Islam or another, don't go there. All your friends will see is the chip on your shoulder, not Christ's love. Remember, as Christ draws and changes Muslims' hearts, their outward situation will change, too. Flinging off a headscarf means nothing, if the veil of Islam is not first removed from their eyes and heart.

One last Q: *People hold conversations with a variety of attitudes: dominance, know-it-all, pleading, humility, etc. Some you would obviously not use, but what is best?*

A: The best "tone" of conversation, if you will, is simple, straight-forward confidence. You should not only live with, but speak with a healthy dose of humility, as well. Simply keep in mind the fact that you could very well **be** your Muslim neighbor instead of the one talking to him. You should be able to approach every opportunity to speak with them and cultivate friendship with a humble gratitude toward the Lord.

Humility doesn't mean you speak with your head down as if you were a servant or somehow subservient to your neighbor. It simply means that you always keep in mind that you have nothing but what has been given to you. You have been given the gift of life —it is not your own and nothing which you have ever done or can lay claim to is truly "yours." You are Christ's servant. Bow your head before Him as you walk forward, boldly proclaiming His Truth.

Regarding the other postures of conversation:

An air of dominance will simply walk you into the quagmire of debate, from which there will be very little hope of escape.

A know-it-all attitude will put off those you are speaking with. Remember that your Muslim friend has a wealth of information to teach you, as well. Your conversation should be one of open-minded learning with you pointing them toward the Truth.

Finally, there is no reason to speak with a pleading attitude. You are not trying to sell them a vacuum cleaner. The Holy Spirit will draw them; no amount of pleading on your part will do that.

Chapter 5

Stereotypes and Misconceptions

Whether you realize it or not, there are numerous stereotypes and misconceptions that inform your Muslim
friends about you —and just as many informing you
about them. In the next few pages, I will list some of
the stereotypes you will encounter about yourself
and those that you might not even be aware of
believing about Muslims. I will list stereotypes that can
have the potential to help in relationship building
and those that will hinder if not corrected.

Stereotypes about YOU

1. All westerners are Christian —Helpful!

This is one stereotype which I have been thankful
for on more than one occasion. Most of my Muslim
friends assumed when they met me that because I
am a westerner I am also a Christian. This assumption
does several things. First, it immediately puts them
on high alert to watch for the other stereotypes they

have heard about westerners (ones I will elaborate upon below).

When they begin to notice a difference in me as opposed to what they have seen in (or heard about) other westerners, questions naturally arise centered on why I am different. This one stereotype has positively opened many doors to share the gospel, born out of my friends' natural curiosity.

2. All Christians drink alcohol and eat pork —Not Helpful

To Muslims, alcohol represents debauchery and pork is the same as eating something found in the sidewalk gutter —it is vile and unclean. There are no "grey" areas here. Muslims take the alcohol so seriously that they will not use vanilla flavoring if it contains any alcohol. Grocery stores in the Muslim world have special "western" sections (think of a store within a store) with a closing door to separate non-Halal meat (i.e. pork) from the meat that Muslims can eat. So what should you do about these two issues?

I am aware in writing this that there are many opinions out there regarding this topic. What follows is a Biblical explanation of how to approach it and some words of caution from one who has lived among the people you desire to reach.

Alcohol: If you sincerely desire to reach your Muslim neighbors and you drink, you will need to refrain.

Now I know those of you reading this who claim to drink wine "for your stomach's sake" will start to object. But please, hear me out! Medicinal purposes aside, there is no real "need" for that glass of wine or cold one during a game. If you desire to reach a people who live by a stricture of rules, you will need to "become all things" and that means abstaining from alcohol.

Yes, there is liberty in Christ but if you are truly struggling with the idea of giving up alcohol in order to have a greater witness, let me ask you this: is alcohol a liberality from which you can abstain or has it become "sin so that grace may abound"? There ought to be nothing in our lives that withholds us from reaching out to those around us for the gospel. When it comes to alcohol, just give it up.

Pork: This one is easier than alcohol. Don't serve it to your Muslim friends and don't eat it around them. Again, this is a bit of an abstinence issue, but not that big of a deal. If they ask you whether you eat pork, be honest. Go straight to the Bible about what you eat and why. Jesus fulfilled the law and prophets and has made the unclean clean. He has given us food to enjoy and pork is part of that.

We are no longer under a law we must fulfill, Jesus did that for us. Not eating pork was part of the law; it is not a commandment. You can also reference Peter's testimony when he was called to visit the gentiles in Caesarea and was told by God in a vision that he was no longer to call that which God has sanctified, "unclean" (Acts 10).

Back to Alcohol. One Final Word: For any arguments that rise to your mind after the discussion of pork and why it is permissible, consider the following verses:

I Corinthians 6:12 "All things are lawful unto me, but all things are not expedient: all things are lawful for me, but I will not be brought under the power of any.

I Corinthians 10:23 "All things are lawful for me, but all things are not expedient: all things are lawful for me, but all things edify not."

Neither alcohol, nor pork for that matter, should be a big enough issue that you are actually arguing with what has been written here. Do you want to reach Muslims? Then become all things and abstain.

Finally, do Muslims ever drink? Yes. In secret, to their shame, and to the shame of their families. Alcohol is never ever seen as something good, holy, or righteous.

3. All Christians Dress Immodestly —Not Helpful

This is another area that, depending on where you live, can be a bit touchy. I will simply ask you to use wisdom with this one. Muslims **will** watch you —I promise you that. They will watch how you interact with your friends, your spouse, your boss. They will watch how you dress, how you eat, how you live on a day-to-day basis. To be honest, this is one of the things I love about living where I do. People watch me all the time —whether I am distinctly aware of it or not— and you know what they see? Jesus! As you live for the Lord, those around you will not be able to help but notice the sweet Spirit of the Lord Jesus Christ that resides within you.

So why a talk on modesty? Because if there is one thing that causes Muslims to label you as someone who does not fear God, it is this. I understand that modes of dress are typically different from someone living in sunny Southern California as opposed to the windy Mid-West, however, there are a few guidelines all can follow. This topic obviously carries the most weight with women, but men, there are a few tips for you, here, too.

Women: Please, and yes, I'm talking to you in Southern California, too, please keep your shoulders covered. No spaghetti strap dresses or tops. Keep your neckline up and your hemline down. No one needs to see your midriff or anything that a low-cut top could possibly reveal. If you can't sit down in your skirt or dress without tugging it to make sure it will cover what is underneath, just don't wear it.

I am well aware that many of you are probably mentally searching through your wardrobe right now, but do know, it makes a difference! Remember that conversation I had with Aisha (Conversation 2 from Chapter 3)? She was led to ask questions about what

I believe and why because of the way I dressed. I'm not telling you to wear a headscarf —in fact, don't! But do dress in a way that you will not have to sec-ond-guess yourself around people who usually cover completely when outside their houses (even if their Western equivalent is long sleeves, a long top, and pants instead of the full, black robe women usually wear).

Men: The exhortation is shorter for you. I'll just give you a few tips. Arab men typically dress with a bit of flare and usually look like they are ready for a busi-ness meeting at the drop of a hat. Keep your "rat-tier" clothing in the closet, especially if you are going to visit them. If your neighbors happen to pop over to your house and you're in your beat-up sweatshirt and holey jeans, don't sweat it. But don't ever go visiting them in their house that way. Your actions (or lack thereof) would be seen as extremely rude.

If you realize that they are coming over for a long-ish visit you might want to change into something a bit more respectable. If you had invited your friends over, change before they arrive. Dress like you are inviting your in-laws for supper. Polo-type shirts and a pair of slacks or **nice** jeans are perfect. Dressing well for your Muslim friends is simply one way of showing them that you value their friendship.

4. All Christians Do Not Pray or Reverence their Holy Book —Can be Helpful

Prayer: Due to a Muslim's outward show and scripted times of prayer, a common misconception regarding Christians is that we do not pray. To their way of thinking, we have no "five-time-a-day" schedule, nor do we pull out a prayer rug and chant memorized words. Therefore, we must not pray.

This misconception can actually be quite helpful. When you do pray, for example, before a meal, and you include a prayer for them because they are going through a hard time, they will be pleasantly surprised. (It is best to ask first, but most Muslims will gladly accept prayer.) And then they will probably ask you about it.

Openly praying and talking about prayer will give you a great opportunity to explain that your prayers are not memorized words, but rather a conversation. Prayer is you talking with the God you know and love. This concept of prayer is very different from what they know and it will draw them to the God who would so lovingly condescend to know us.

Reverencing the Bible: My one exhortation is this: please do not ever place your Bible on the floor. This is seen as extreme disrespect toward something which is holy. If you underline or mark verses in your Bible, explain to your Muslim friends why if they ask.

It is better to have an un-marked Bible which you can read with your Muslim friend should the occasion arise, as marking a holy book is seen as disrespectful, as well. If you do not have a "clean" Bible, however, just tell them why you mark in it —because as you read, God shows you things about Himself and you want to remember those things, so you highlight or underline that passage to help you remember.

Stereotypes about THEM

1. All Arabs ride camels and live in the desert in tents —Can be Helpful

If you approach this one with a high-and-mighty we-haven't-been-nomads-in-centuries attitude, your conversation will obviously go nowhere fast. But if you use this as a launching point for further discussion about who they really are and where they have come from, it can help your friendship grow deeper.

Arabs, especially those living transplanted lives in the west, love when they are asked about their homeland. Arab lands have a long and rich history which most Arabs are more than willing to talk about. If you want to know about your friends, all you need to do is ask them where they or their family came from. In reality, most Arabs haven't lived in tents, ridden camels, or lived in the dessert for years upon years.

Camels are trotted out for shows and tourists who still falsely believe that camels are the number one mode of transportation. Let me put that notion to rest: 99% of the Arab world no longer need camels as their mode of transportation —just like we no longer ride everywhere on horseback.

2. All Muslims Hate the West —Not Helpful

If you approach your impending friendship with this attitude, your friendship won't develop very well. Just as you should despise the view that all Christians live a debauched life of immorality and drinking, they despise this opinion. Now I won't say that it isn't true for some, but it is highly likely that your neighbors aren't ones who hold such an opinion. And if they do, it might be because of how they have been treated thus far. Treat them as Christ would —as a person who has been created and is loved by Him— and their opinion of America might change, as well. Many a time Muslim friends have been surprised to find that I am American because I am "so different" from what they have seen or heard.

3. All Muslims are Terrorists —Not Helpful

Similarly to stereotype number 2, it would not be wise to approach any friendship with this idea in the back of your mind. If you want to "win them" for Christ, approach your friendship with loads of love, patience, and desire to understand where they are coming from (both geographically and in mind-set). I hope it would go without saying that if you approach a friendship thinking that they're going to murder you in your sleep, your friendship won't have very solid ground upon which to be built.

Muslims want to be taken seriously and appreci-
ated for who they are as people —just like we do. So
respect them for who they are. Many hold respectable positions as doctors, specialists, and owners
of varying businesses both local and in their home
country. Get to know them. Don't assume.

And who knows? If they really are, maybe they'll turn
to Christ because of your witness before they carry
out their jihadist mission!

4. Two more for the road: All Arabs are Muslims and are married to more than one wife.

Arab = Muslim is simply a misnomer. Many Arabs
from Egypt, Lebanon, Jordan, and even Iraq are
"historically" Christian. They are not Muslims and are
severely persecuted because of their background
and history. As such, they may flee from their homeland and seek refuge in the United States. If that is
the case, they are often separated from everything
they knew and loved (possibly even their families).
Love them with the love Christ has given you. Their
understandings may be different, but that can be
discussed openly with "Orthodox" or "Coptic" Christians from these areas of the world. They will be more
than happy and likely will be thrilled to find a believer
in Jesus who wants to be their friend.

Remember that Americans who discriminate against
Muslims often will not be able to tell the difference

between Muslim Arabs and Christian Arabs. These persecuted Arabs face persecution in their homeland because of their beliefs and from Americans (or other westerners where they have decided to live) because of the color of their hair, eyes, and skin.

Muslim = married to multiple women can also be a misconception. Yes, the Qur'an allows it. Yes, many Muslims are married to more than one wife. But there are also many Muslim families who only have one wife. Good friends of mine have no children and are deeply in love with each other. The husband wouldn't dream of marrying another woman —he is deeply in love with his one wife.

Don't assume that all females living in a household are one man's wives. They may be, but if this is the case, the husband will tell you and often will be proud of the fact. Discussion over this issue can be held as you become friends. If they have one wife and confide to you that they are considering marrying another, by all means, give wise council from the scriptures and advise them to not do so (Mark 10:7; Matthew 19:5; Ephesians 5:31).

A Final Thought

Try to keep as open a mind as possible when getting to know your friends. Western media has done much to demonize Muslims. Though much of what is said about atrocities committed in the name of

PASTOR KEVIN
(509) 697-7833

Islam is correct and condoned by the Qur'an, do not assume your neighbors fall into that category. For you to automatically assume that your Muslim neighbors are terrorists is like them believing that you personally want to take all Arab lands and rule them in the name of imperialism.

Chapter 6

A Living Testimony

It has often been repeated among Christian circles that the only Bible some people will read is the one written by your life. When reaching out to those around you for the purpose of sharing the gospel, I cannot stress how absolutely true this is. In this chapter, I will highlight several areas of your living testimony that will be especially powerful to Muslims who may be reading the "Bible" of your life.

1. Husband/Wife Relationships

For those of you who are married, the relationship you share with your spouse can serve as a veritable beacon of light when it comes to your Christian testimony. Muslim marriages, though sometimes built from, and through, love, often are devoid of the principles which Christ gives to guide us in our relationships with one another. The daily loving, caring, concern, respect, honoring, and helping of your spouse —out of love for Christ— does not occur inside the Muslim home. Yes, respect, honor, and deference will often be shown to the husband by the wife, but rarely is the case reversed and rarer still is it done out of love.

Husbands: Love your wife by practically demonstrating this when your Muslim friends come over. Help her clear the table or wash dishes (yes, even when your guest is there!), make the lunch so your wife can be free to speak with your guest's wife. Think of practical and obvious things that you could do for her. Even if it is not serving dinner all by yourself, perhaps you could dish out desert or after-dinner tea or coffee. Be sure to portray the fact that, in Christ, your wife is your helpmeet, not a subservient slave.

Wives: Love your husband by verbally respecting him in front of your guests. Talk him up —tell your guest how loving and wonderful your husband is. Tell her of all the things he does for you and why you respect him. Tell her why you love him so much. A love marriage in Christ is vastly different from all others —and it should appear so! Don't be bashful —talk about your man! Be careful with joking about him —what could be taken as a joke with western company could be seen as rude and disrespectful to eastern guests. Verbally express respect for your husband.

An Example: The husband of a Muslim family accepted Christ as his Saviour. He desired that his wife would join him in his newfound faith. Rather than preach at her, he was advised to simply love her in the way Jesus instructs. Two months went by and, as the husband demonstrated more of Christ's love to his wife, his wife started to ask questions about this Jesus he now worshipped. Finally, she, too, gave her life to Jesus Christ.

When asked what drew her to seek Christ, she talked about her husband. "When I saw him clearing the supper dishes, I knew he was a changed man. Before this, he never would have helped me with housework. But now he helps clear the table, does dishes for me sometimes, and even brings me breakfast in bed! This is a man who loves me now. I wanted to know why he had this love in him."

When the husband was asked what first drew him to Christ he said, "My next door neighbors were missionaries. We would often spend time at their house. I watched my friend do things for his wife that I would never dream of doing for mine. When I ask him why he served his wife instead of letting her serve him, he taught me about Jesus."

2. Well Behaved and Disciplined Children

Arab families **love** children. Many homes will see children running wildly through them, shouting and chasing each other, as their parents and parents' friends look on. Whenever there are social gatherings, children are almost always included and are seen as a blessing, not a nuisance —no matter how rowdy they may get. That said, these children are often lacking manners and discipline.

When Muslim families are introduced to you and
your children, one of the first comments you might
hear is how beautiful they are (if they are young) or
grown-up looking (if older). However, as you get to
know your neighbors, your friends will soon wonder
what "magic elixir" you have discovered that keeps
your children from acting wild and actually answer-
ing "yes ma'am" to your request. Your new Muslim
friends will be more than happy to have you and
your children over to their house as often as you'd
like —they are hoping that your children's good
behavior will be a positive influence on their children's bad.

As questions or statements of amazement are
offered up in response to your well-behaved children, you have the opportunity to explain your meth-
ods of discipline and the reasons behind them. You
can open up the Bible and discuss verses about your
God-given responsibility to discipline your children.
Those verses can then lead to discussion from the
New Testament about God loving his children and
disciplining them.

What if they are not so well behaved? Or what if
they decide to act out when your neighbors are
over? Remind your child that discipline will be
coming **after** the neighbors go home or **after** you
return to yours from visiting theirs. There is no reason
to discipline them in front of strangers and is probably not a good idea. But remain consistent with

your child and feel free to let them know (in front of your guests) that discipline will be coming. Hold them accountable for their actions.

3. Interactions with Friends

One stereotype that perhaps should have been mentioned earlier, is that all westerners (and yes, that means Christians) are lose and immoral. Your interactions with those around you can either give rise to further belief in this stereotype, or a realization of its falsehood.

Women: When interacting with men, as often occurs in the western world, try to be aware of your proximity to members of the opposite sex. If you're with your Muslim friends and you're all hanging out with a big group, try to make sure there is a healthy distance between you and a guy friend. It's okay to talk with them —I'm not asking you to change who you are— but keep some distance there. If you're married, then stick with your husband or the females in a group. Talking with the husband of another woman or an unmarried man is probably not the best idea. There will always be exceptions to this, but when getting to know your new Muslim friends err on the side of caution.

Guys: The same as is written above goes for you. When hanging out with Muslim friends, stick with guys. Let your wife go off with the women and you stick with men. It's proper, makes sense, and keeps you out of trouble. By safeguarding yourself from appearing to flirt or engage inappropriately with members of the opposite sex, you are sending a loud-and-clear message to your Muslim friends that you fear God.

4. What You "Do"

Believe it or not, your friends will watch everything you do. What you do at work, on your off time, with friends, even in your home can be noted and repeated by curious onlookers. Your life is an open book and that's a good thing (remember they're reading the Bible of your life!).

Questions about what type of job you hold, how you spend your money, how much money you earn, when you want to retire, whether you want to move some day, and why you take your wife on date nights are just a few of the questions you can expect. None of those questions are meant as rude ones (remember, question asking etiquette is not the same in Arab cultures); your neighbors/friends are just curious as to the varying details and aspects of your life.

Think through what you do and why. Be ready to give every man a reason for the hope that is in you —and your motivation for life. Try not to take offense at questions asked; your friends are just curious about you and what makes you the way you are. The more honest you can be the better (including telling them that your salary is culturally too personal to disclose).

They will slowly but surely build a picture of who you are. The goal is that they will see you living life motivated in every way by a sincere love for Christ. Remember, we are called to do ALL things —even if that is just **eating** or **drinking**— to the glory of Christ Jesus our Lord.

5. Where You "Go"

This is an aspect of your life that holds great potential for relationship building. Your friends will be curious about your goings out and comings in whether they come right out and say it or not. Where you go on Sunday (and why), what kind of family vacations you take, where you take your wife on date night, why you go to church on Wednesday, what a prayer meeting is, and why you get together with a bunch of ladies for a "coffee morning" will run through their mind.

Again, be honest, be open, and if all possible, invite them to "go" along with you! I am not telling you to invite them on your family vacation, but leave the invitation wide open for church on Sunday, Bible study on Wednesday, your lady's or men's book club, a kids' play-date, or other event that would be open to receiving visitors. Try to include them in the "goings on" in your life. The more time they are able to spend with you, the more they will be able to understand what you do, who you are, and why.

Chapter 7

Pointing to Jesus

As you get to know your Muslim friends, there could very well be a point when discussion focuses more consistently on the Bible. Introducing Muslims to Jesus through the New Testament often produces more futility than profitable discussion. Muslims take very little stock in the New Testament. They are, however, more inclined to listen if you begin with scripture from the Old Testament (notice I say **begin** with —never leave out the New Testament; it's the fulfillment of the Old!) Many of the prophets we are familiar with are also considered prophets in Islam. Men like Adam, Noah, Abraham, Moses, and David are very familiar to Muslims and are good starting points for sharing the gospel.

In this chapter, you will find an explanation of how to use seven Old Testament prophets as a starting point to share the gospel. Familiarize yourself with these passages before you discuss them. I cannot stress enough how crucial they are to understanding Christ and His work on earth. Think back to the two disciples on their way to Emmaus for a moment. Jesus met

with them and began speaking about His recent
death and resurrection. How did He do it? "...begin-
ning at Moses and all the prophets, he expounded
unto them in all the scriptures the things concerning
himself" (Luke 24:27).

Adam

Explain to your friend that sin entered the world
through Adam. By one man's sin, the human race
became cursed and separated from relationship
with God. Read chapter 3 of Genesis to drive home
these points. Finally, show your friend that God promised a future Redeemer to crush Satan and sin: "And
I will put enmity between thee and the woman, and
between thy seed and her seed; it shall bruise thy
head, and thou shalt bruise his heel" Genesis 3:14.

Noah

The story of Noah's life helps reveal God's plan of
salvation for all humankind. Read the entire story
of Noah with your friend if possible, highlighting the
aspect of God's specific instructions for their salvation. Just as there was only one way to save Noah
and his family, so, too, God would provide one way
to save us from sin and hell.

Abraham

God revealed that a Saviour would come "through"
Abraham —from his family line. Read Genesis 22:1-18

to give your friends the full effect of this piece of the puzzle. Let the aspect of a God-provided sacrifice surface in your discussion. It's not necessarily something you need to discuss in detail, but draw their attention to it. Let the parallel to the gospel arise at every possible opportunity.

Important Note: Muslims believe that it was Ishmael, not Isaac, who was sacrificed. Avoid pointless argumentation about the whole thing and simply read the Bible passages. The scriptures will speak for themselves. If your friends tell you that the recorded story of Isaac being sacrificed is proof that the Bible has been changed, remember what we discussed before and simply tell them that the oldest Bibles in existence have this exact story. Maybe it was not the Bible that was changed....

Moses

Moses was given the law by God and was also given prophecy about a future Prophet. The law, you explain to your friend, was **not** given to Moses to show us how to live perfectly. We cannot, after all, do anything perfectly. It **was**, however, given to show us that we need a Saviour.

God's standard for His people is perfection. We cannot possibly hope to attain that lofty goal. How will we ever be able to stand before Him?

The answer, you tell your Muslim friend, is in the future

Prophet of whom Moses spoke. In Deuteronomy 18:15, we are told, "The LORD thy God will raise up unto thee a Prophet from the midst of thee, of thy brethren, like unto me; unto him ye shall hearken." Your Muslim friend will possibly interject and tell you that this prophet is Muhammad (peace be upon him). Tell your friend that you would like to discuss some other scriptures about this Prophet and see what they say. As you continue through other key Biblical figures, it will become blatantly obvious that Muhammad was not the Prophet spoken of in this passage.

David

Through David, God promised His kingdom would be established without end and that He would rule over the ends of the earth.

Go to II Samuel 7:16, 29 and explain that David was promised by God that his kingdom would be an everlasting kingdom. The everlasting kingdom refers to God's kingdom and the continuing promise that a Saviour would come, a Saviour which would rule over the whole earth, a Saviour who would live perfectly, who would suffer for us and take the punishment for our sin.

Read all of Psalm 22 with your friend. Preface your read-through with the fact that this Psalm is talk-ing about the coming Saviour. Discuss the varying themes within the chapter: vs. 1-18 suffering, vs. 19-22

salvation in God, vs. 23-24 the Saviour's identifica-
tion with suffering, vs. 25-26 mankind saved through
the Saviour, and vs. 27-28 the Saviour will govern and
reign over the world.

Read Psalm 130 and again discuss the theme of
salvation.

Isaiah

Isaiah is a literal gold mine of Old Testament gospel-
directed scriptures and prophecy. These are the
scriptures that will most effectively help Muslims realize that the prophesied One to come is not Muhammad. In this section I have listed verse references
along with a short explanation detailing main points
to discuss.

Isaiah 7:14 – A sign given to all people: a virgin con-
ceiving and bearing Immanuel. Immanuel = God
WITH us!

Isaiah 9:1, 6 – Prophecy pertaining to the coming
Saviour, Immanuel, God **with** us. These verses discuss:
1) What lands He would traverse (v.1, 2). 2) His King-
ship (v. 6 a, b). 3) His lineage (v. 6 c).

Isaiah 11:1-5 – The Saviour's lineage is alluded to in
v. 1. The rest of the verses pertain to what the Saviour will do. Notice that His **actions** are prophesied
here: He will perfectly understand how to live, He
will judge the poor with righteousness, He will smite

the earth with the rod of his **mouth** (i.e. with words, not swords!). The fact that the Saviour 's actions are prophesied is something you might want to point out to your friend. Later when discussing Jesus, they will have these verses in their mind to weigh Him (and Muhammad) against. John 8:15-16 records Jesus' words about His method of judgment and pairs with this portion of scripture extremely well.

Isaiah 12:1-6 – This is a beautiful portion of scripture to read with your friend. Whereas salvation is never assured in Islam, here Isaiah pens an entire chapter in praise to the Lord for His Salvation. In verse 2 Isaiah says twice that **God** is and has become his salvation. In verse 3 he speaks of drawing water "out of the wells of salvation." This is a specific verse to keep in mind when looking through the New Testament. Return to this portion when reading Jesus' words to the Samaritan woman in John 4:10 and 14, "Jesus answered and said unto her, If thou knewest the gift of God, and who it is that saith to thee, Give me to drink; thou wouldest have asked of him, and he would have given thee living water…. But whosoever drinketh of the water that I shall give him shall never thirst; but the water that I shall give him shall be in him a well of water springing up into everlasting life."

Isaiah 28:16 – Jesus used these words in reference to Himself. Make your friend aware of this fact. Eventually discuss Jesus' words in Matthew 21:33-46 and come back to this verse. He is the cornerstone that the builders rejected.

Isaiah 29:18-19 – Things only a Saviour could do. Specifically point out the fact that the deaf will hear and the blind will see. Point out that what they would **hear** and **see** is the Word of God! This will be useful later when reading through John when Jesus is referred to as the Word that became flesh.

Isaiah 35:3-6 – This is another passage which refers to the actions of the Saviour . Blind eyes will be open, lame men will leap, the dumb will speak. When John's disciples came to Jesus and asked if He were the "one that should come" (i.e. the Saviour) or if they should look for another, Jesus answered them by saying, "...Go and shew John again those things which ye do hear and see: the blind receive their sight, and the lame walk, the lepers are cleansed, and the deaf hear, the dead are raised up, and the poor have the gospel preached to them" Matthew 11:4-5.

Isaiah 40:3 – This is a verse to keep in mind for when your discussions bring you to Jesus. Jesus quoted this in reference to John.

Isaiah 40:5-8 – Three points to bring to your friend's attention. 1) The glory of the LORD would be revealed (many of the "men of old" had seen the glory of God —specifically Moses— but never had it been revealed or made known to all people) 2) People are grass, the Word is eternal. 3) Jesus is referred to as the Word of God (Jn. 1).

Isaiah 42:1-9 – This again speaks of the Servant Saviour, and His actions. The Saviour will be a light; He will open blind eyes and set prisoners free from darkness.

Isaiah 43:10-13 – This works powerfully in conjunction with the entirety of John 8. Read the passage from Isaiah and then read through John 8, where Jesus' words regarding who He is are recorded. Verse 58 and 59 are very powerful.

Isaiah 45:18 – This verse also works well with John 8. Another New Testament portion to read is John 10: 27-31 where the people want to stone Jesus because He says He IS God. He says that He and God are ONE. This is very important to point out, because many Muslims think that Christians believe in three gods (the Father and Son of which are two). Stress the fact that we believe in ONE God.

Isaiah 52:3 – Prophecy of redemption.

Isaiah 52:13-15 – Prophecy of the redeemer.

Isaiah 53 – The whole chapter speaks of the One who will come and redeem the nations — not with money but blood (vs. 11). It is impossible to thoroughly articulate how many uses there are for this chapter. Read it and read it again. Become intimately familiar with this portion and be ready to use it as much as possible.

Isaiah 61:1-3 – Jesus said this prophecy was FULFILLED

in HIM! Point this out to your Muslim friend. Go to Luke 4:15-21 and read through the passage.

Isaiah 64:6 – This is a great verse to use in reference to sin and need for a Saviour.

Isaiah 65:1 – Here, the prophesy is foretold that all people, regardless of language or nationality, would be welcomed to come through God's plan of salvation. Even those who "asked not for me" would behold Him.

Isaiah 65:9 – Again, the "seed" is spoken of, a Saviour, an "inheritor of my mountains," a King who shall rule over it.

Isaiah 66:23 – This is an important verse to read, as God clearly declares that ALL people will come to worship him. His salvation is for ALL people.

Micah

Micah's words in Micah 5:2 relate **specifically** to where the Messiah would be born. This is a great verse to use if Muslims believe that Muhammad is the One to come. Muhammad was not born in Bethlehem; he was born in Mecca.

In a Nut Shell

Adam: Seed of the woman would crush the head of the serpent.

Noah: God built an ark to save humanity; God prepares a way to save us from sin.

Abraham: God said He would bless Abraham with many descendants and that through Him all the peoples of the world would be blessed. The Saviour will come through Abraham.

Moses: The law reveals our need for a Saviour. Prophecy in Deuteronomy 18:15 states there would be a prophet to lead all people.

David: God promised that His kingdom would be established through David, a kingdom without end, ruling over the ends of the earth.

Isaiah: Prophesies of the future Messiah.

Micah: Prophesies the precise location of birth for the Messiah.

Chapter 8

Jesus Himself

On to the New Testament! Knowing your New Testament is just as important as knowing your Old. They are two pieces to a perfectly crafted puzzle —each needs the other to form a whole picture. If you are able to give your Muslim friends a clear picture of the Messiah as prophesied in the Old Testament, it will make the discussion of the New Testament all the clearer and easier to be understood. When read in context of the Old Testament, Jesus' rightful identity as God comes leaping off the pages of Scripture.

In this section I have outlined parts of Jesus' life which correspond to what you have already read in the Old Testament. Jesus' fulfillment of prophecy is included, as are quotes from Jesus and those closest to Him affirming his deity. As with the previous chapter, this is not something you necessarily want to rush through. Each portion could be used as a topic for Bible study or lengthy conversation. The most important thing to do is simply get your friends reading the Word of God. Please keep in mind that this is by no means an exhaustive list of scripture verses you can use!

The WORD of God

John 1 is one of the most beneficial portions of scripture when explaining Jesus to your Muslim friends. Much of the jargon we use and are familiar with is downright confusing to Muslims. Points of confusion can be explained, but starting here will help them understand Jesus in a way that bypasses much of that confusion.

As you read through each verse, highlight the following important points:

Verse 1: "In the beginning was the Word, and the Word was with God, and the Word was God."

- Word of God = God Himself.

Verse 2: "The same was in the beginning with God."

- Word of God/God Himself always was. He is the I AM.

Verse 3: "All things were made by him; and without him was not anything made that was made."

- Word of God/God Himself = Creator

Verse 4: "In him was life; and the life was the light of men."

- Word of God = Giver of Life = Light of the world

Verse 5: "And the light shineth in darkness; and the darkness comprehended it not."

- The Light of the world shines IN darkness = God came to earth

Verse 6-8: John explains himself

- Sent of God to bear witness of the Light that all men might believe

Verse 9: "That was the true Light, which lighteth every man that cometh into the world."

- The Light (God) "lighteth" every man = gives life to every man (reference verse 4)

Verse 10: "He was in the world, and the world was made by him, and the world knew him not."

He, the Light, GOD, was IN the world. In case any clarification is needed, the world was made by Him leaving no doubt whatsoever. The "He" that came into the world is God Himself and none other.

Verse 11: "He came unto his own, and his own received him not."

Reference back to Genesis 22 and remind your friend that the Messiah would come through Abraham. Therefore, when His "own" received Him not,

He is talking about Abraham's descendants to whom Jesus came in the flesh.

Verse 12-13: "But as many as received him, to them gave he power to become the sons of God, even to them that believe on his name. Which were born, not of blood, nor of the will of the flesh, nor of the will of man, but of God."

Who has the power to grant this "son-ship" other than God Himself?

Verse 14: "And the Word was made flesh, and dwelt among us, (and we beheld his glory, the glory as of the only begotten of the Father,) full of grace and truth."

Go back to Isaiah 53:2 and remind your friend that the Saviour was prophesied to "grow up before him as a tender plant, and as a root out of a dry ground…"

Isaiah 11:1-2 is another one to revisit, "And there shall come forth a rod out of the stem of Jesse, and a Branch shall grow out of his roots: and the spirit of the LORD shall rest upon him, the spirit of wisdom and understanding, the spirit of counsel and might, the spirit of knowledge and of the fear of the Lord…"

Jesus Himself

After reading John 1:1-14, start to introduce your friends to the words of Jesus.

Luke 2: God's Work

From the earliest moments, Jesus makes it abun-
dantly clear that He is on earth for one purpose: to
reveal God. In Luke 2 the story is recorded of Jesus'
visit to the temple during and after a feast. Unbe-
knownst to his parents, He remained in Jerusalem
while his company began their journey home. After a
day on the road, Jesus' mother and father returned
to Jerusalem to look for Him.

They found Him after three days, "...in the temple,
sitting in the midst of the doctors, both hearing them,
and asking them questions" (v. 46). The people
there "...were astonished at his understanding and
answers" (v. 47). Obviously distraught, Mary asks
Jesus why He had stayed behind to which Jesus
replied, "How is it that ye sought me? Wist ye not
that I must be about my Father's business?" (v. 49)
His earthy father, Joseph, was a carpenter. He had
no business in the temple beyond the sacrifices and
feast days in worship to God. The Father Jesus is talking about is God Himself. And from John 1, we know
that the Father IS God. So Jesus is saying He must be
about God's business.

Luke 4: Prophecy Fulfilled

Fast-forward a chapter and Jesus is all grown up. He
continues to live among His people and one day He
enters into the synagogue. He is handed the scrolls

and does the most extraordinary thing: He proclaims to the people that He is the Messiah, the One to preach freedom from sin.

Luke 4:16-21: "And he came to Nazareth, where he had been brought up: and, as his custom was, he went into the synagogue on the Sabbath day, and stood up for to read. And there was delivered unto him the book of the prophet Esaias. And when he had opened the book, he found the place where it was written, The Spirit of the Lord is upon me, because he hath anointed me to preach the gospel to the poor; he hath sent me to heal the broken-hearted, to preach deliverance to the captives, and recovering of sight to the blind, to set at liberty them that are bruised, to preach the acceptable year of the Lord. And he closed the book, and he gave it again to the minister, and sat down. And the eyes of all them that were in the synagogue were fastened on him. And he began to say unto them, This day is this scripture fulfilled in your ears." Jesus is claiming to be the One to come that Isaiah foretold!

Luke 5: Sin Forgiven

This chapter holds yet another key to the identity of Jesus. Early in the chapter we see Him healing (verse12-15) but that's not the most amazing part. Fast forward to verse 18 and read through verse 26. Here, Jesus declares something only God could rightfully declare —that a man's sins are forgiven! He not only declares it so, but follows up this amazing declaration with a miracle to confirm it. The religious leaders rightly asked, "Who is this which speaketh blasphemies? Who can forgive sins, but God alone?" (v. 21). This, my friend, is the point! Who indeed! Only God has that power and Jesus is declaring it so. He is declaring for all to know that HE is GOD.

Luke 7: Prophecy Fulfilled (again)

In verses 19-22 John has his disciples ask Jesus to clarify if He is, in fact, "he that should come." Jesus points straight to the prophecies and says, "Go your way, and tell John what things ye have seen and heard; how that the blind see, the lame walk, the lepers are cleansed, the deaf hear, the dead are raised, to the poor the gospel is preached. And blessed is he, whosoever shall not be offended in me." He is saying in no uncertain terms, YES, I AM HE.

Luke 8: Power to Heal

Throughout the Bible, stories of healings are recorded. Prophets of old were sent by God to heal a person who had called upon God. In each and every situation, the prophet is indebted to call upon God, to seek Him, to point everyone's attention to the Lord of Heaven that glory might be given where it is due. In absolutely NO case whatsoever do we see glory being given to the prophet Himself. Except in one case: when Jesus does the healing.

In Luke 8:41-56 we read of a double miracle, that of a woman who had an issue of blood and a little girl who was on her deathbed. In the case of the woman with an issue of blood, the Bible records that Jesus knew someone touched Him because "virtue is gone out" of Him (v. 46). He did not call down healing power from heaven, it was wholly contained **within** Him. He was the healing power. And when the story came fully into the light, Jesus declared that her faith **in Him** had made her whole! FAITH IN HIM! Not in any other. This either amounts to blasphemy or absolute affirmation that Jesus truly, accurately, 100% IS God.

The same attribution is asserted in verses 49-56 with the little girl who was dying. Jesus told the Father to believe only and she would be well. And when she was raised back to life, Jesus **commanded** it to happen. He uttered two words: "Maid, arise." There was no asking God for help, just a simple commanding it to be. Only God has this power.

Luke 9: Prophecy Affirmed and Foretold

From your foray into the prophecies of Isaiah, you have come to realize that the Messiah, the Saviour, is prophesied to have suffered. In Luke 9, Jesus affirms this prophecy and declares to his disciples that it **will** happen —to Him!

In verses 18-22, Jesus asks his disciples what people are saying of Him. They report that some said He was

John the Baptist, some Isaiah, and some one of the prophets risen from the dead. Then Jesus asks them who they believe Him to be. Peter declares outright that he believes Jesus is "The Christ of God" (v. 20). Jesus gives a verbal affirmation to this statement and declares that all of the prophecies He has fulfilled are not finished yet. There is yet a prophecy He will fulfill and it is the prophecy of the Suffering Servant.

As is noted time after time in Isaiah, "The Son of man must suffer many things, and be rejected of the elders and chief priests and scribes, and be slain, and be raised the third day" (v.22). One of the most astounding statements in that verse is that He will be **raised.** The Suffering Servant will not just suffer, not just face rejection and death, but will be **raised!** He will be the **living** Messiah, the Saviour of the World, to whom will belong an **everlasting** kingdom, reigning over the world without end.

This same prophecy is spoken of and affirmed in Luke 18:31-33.

Luke 21: Be Not Deceived

Fast forward through the book a bit. Here, Jesus tells the people again that He IS the Messiah, the Saviour. Verse 8: "And he said, 'Take heed that ye be not deceived: for many shall come in my name, saying, I am Christ; and the time draweth near: go ye not therefore after them.'" Look again at what He said, "...be not deceived: for many shall come in **my**

name, saying I am Christ…" What name is He claiming? That of Christ!

Luke 22: Thou Sayest

This is a short passage among the trial and subsequent crucifixion of Jesus. During the trial, Pilate asks Him whether He is the King of the Jews. Jesus said, "Thou sayest it." In three words Jesus again affirms that He is the King who should come through the line of David, of the seed of Abraham.

Luke 24: The Risen Christ

In Luke 24, after He was crucified and raised from the dead, Jesus revisits his disciples. During one of these visits, He walked with two of them on the road to Emmaus. These men were understandably confused and distraught regarding the recent occurrences. Jesus answered them simply and thoroughly, maintaining the fact that everything which had occurred was prophecy needing to be fulfilled. Luke 24:25-27 "Then he said unto them, O fools, and slow of heart to believe all that the prophets have spoken: ought not Christ to have suffered these things, and to enter into his glory? And beginning at Moses and all the prophets, he expounded unto them in all the scriptures the things concerning himself."

He affirmed that He was, indeed, the Risen Christ, the Messiah and Saviour. And He affirmed that He was so THROUGH the scriptures. The scripture, He said, pointed to HIM. None other. HE IS MESSIAH.

John 3:10-21: I Have Told You

This is a portion of scripture that takes a couple read-throughs to wrap your mind around. But when you do, the resultant understanding is remarkable. Previously to these few verses, Jesus had told Nicodemus that man needed to be born again in order to see the Kingdom of God (vs. 1-9). Somewhat bewildered, Nicodemus questioned how such a thing could be so. Verses 10-21 are Jesus' reply.

Verse 10-12 – Jesus first asks Nicodemus how he can possibly be a "master of Israel" and not know the things of which Jesus spoke. His query to Nicodemus clearly implies that, as someone who should know the scriptures inside and out, the idea of new life through God should not be unfamiliar.

Verse 13 – This is the verse you'll want to read over several times. This verse is really astounding when you look at it. I fear that it all too often gets overlooked by the more popular and well quoted verses following it, but this is a gem that should be memorized and repeated just as much.

"And no man hath ascended up to heaven, but he that came down from heaven, even the son of man, which is in heaven."

Jesus states clearly that no man hath ascended up to heaven **but** He that came down from heaven.

Who is this one that came down? "...the son of man, which is **in** heaven"! What?? That's right. Jesus is saying in one fell-swoop that the only **man** who ascended into heaven **first** came to earth **from** heaven and is none other than the son of man (the Saviour) which is **in** heaven!

As you have seen from previous verses, Jesus refers to Himself as the son of man. He is therefore saying that He not only descended from heaven but that He did so as a **man** and simultaneously still resides in heaven! Only God could do such a thing! What a verse!

Verse 14-15 – Prophecy that would specifically and pictorially be fulfilled in the Son of Man.

Verse 16-17 – Combine these two verses. Jesus came into the world to SAVE it!

Verse18 – This is an excellent verse for Muslims. Though they may possibly fear condemnation if they decide to believe, they need to realize that they are condemned already because they have not believed in the ONE of whom all prophets spoke!

Verse 19-21 – These will be some hard words for Muslims to deal with. Firstly, they are facing shame and family pressure if they even *think* of converting. Secondly, many believe that they are "good enough" and thus would balk at the idea that they love evil and so are not willing to accept Jesus. These are words to read through, answer questions concerning, and dialogue through, and then let settle in their hearts. Remember that the word will not return void. This is a section to get into their minds and simply let reside there.

John 4:1-26: Living Water

Refer back to Isaiah 12:1-6 when reading through this story. This story occurs between Jesus and a Samaritan woman at a well. She has gone to draw water and meets Jesus there. What Jesus tells her is quite astonishing. Especially focus on the following points with your friend when reading/talking through this story.

1. In verse 10, 12, and 14 Jesus tells the woman that He has living water which, if one were to drink, would spring up unto eternal life.

2. In verse 26 Jesus calls Himself the Messiah!

John 5:16-18, 39, 45-46: Search the Scriptures

Verse 16-18: Here we not only see that Jesus says that He is equal with God, but we are also allowed to see that the people He was speaking to understood that He meant this as well!

Verse 39: Jesus says that the scriptures testify of HIM! The verses that you will have hopefully previously read through with your friend and those which testify of HIM! Every single verse of prophecy about the

Saviour to come is speaking of Jesus Christ!

Verse 45-46: Here Jesus points specifically to Moses and declares that Moses wrote about HIM! Reference Jesus' words in John 3:14 again.

John 6:32-35, 40, 47-51: I Am the Bread of Life

Verse 32-35 – These verses include one of Jesus' "I AM" statements. Here He says that God gives the "bread of life" and Jesus is that bread. Read these verses thoroughly, thoughtfully, and carefully. Several read-throughs of these verses would be beneficial to allow Jesus' statement to fully sink in. He is blatantly saying He is GOD.

Verse 40 – Jesus again states that anyone who believes in HIM will have eternal life. No one can offer such a promise —only God can do that.

Verse 47-51 – A reiteration of the above verses.

John 7:37-39, 42: Come Unto Me

Verse 37-39 – Jesus again refers to the prophecy of living water. He adds a new dimension here and speaks of the Holy Spirit which would come.

Verse 42 – Prophecy fulfilled in Jesus.

John 8:12, 51, 53, 56-59: I Am

The whole chapter is excellent dialogue between Jesus and the Pharisees. The verses I have chosen here are those which should specifically be pointed out and discussed if possible.

Verse 12 – Jesus declares He is the "light of the world."

Verse 51 – This is quite astonishing. Jesus says that if anyone "keeps his saying," i.e. follows and obeys Him, they will never see death! Again, this is something only God could do.

Verse 53, 56-59 – Pharisees issue the paramount question: Are you greater than Abraham? Jesus picks up the gauntlet, looks them straight in the eye and says, "I AM!"

John 9:35-37: It is He

Jesus again, to yet another person, declares the fact that He is God.

John 10:17-18, 25-33: I Lay Down My Life

Verse 17-18 – Jesus speaks of his death and resurrection. This is an excellent verse for Muslims since they believe that Judas was put on the cross in Jesus' place before Jesus died. If Judas had been put on the cross, there would have been no reason for Jesus to speak of the power to both lay down His life and take it again.

Verse 25-33 – Jesus declares Himself to be God by saying: 1. His works testify to the fact and 2. He grants eternal life to those that follow Him. Those around Him react by wanting to stone Him. Why? Because He said He was God (vs. 33).

By now, anyone who has read all of these words of Jesus has only two choices. Either Jesus is an insane madman or indeed, He IS God in the flesh!

John 11:25-26, 49-52: I Am the Resurrection

Verse 25-26 – Believe in Jesus, never die.

Verse 49-52 – Prophecy concerning Jesus' death.

John 14:6-11: I Am the Way

Jesus admonishes his disciples to believe Him. Make note of how He continually affirms the fact that He and the Father are one.

John 15:1-27: I Am the Vine/ I Have Chosen You/ Bear Witness

Through this chapter several things stand out:

1. We can do nothing apart from Jesus (vs. 5)

2. He grants requests (v. 6)

3. He gives joy (v. 11)

4. His example for love is laying one's life down (vs. 12-15) which He will do

5. He chooses (vs. 16)

6. He commands (vs. 17)

7. He fulfilled all prophecy (vs. 25)

8. He will always be testified of (vs. 26-27)

Other New Testament Figures

Though I could include far more in this book, suffice it to say every single story and every single verse written by every single New Testament writer points to Jesus.

"To him give all the prophets witness, that through his name whosoever believeth in him shall receive remission of sins" Acts 10:43.

Chapter 9

Going Deeper and Discipling

At this point, if you have been able to go through most of the above passages and concepts with your Muslim friend, one of a few results will occur. They will disown you as their friend, accept Jesus, or ask you to tell them more. Some Muslims want to know all they can before making any sort of a decision to follow the One you are telling them about. In this chapter you will find discussion topics and verses for "going deeper" and discipling a new believer. Similarly to the two previous chapters, verses will have an explanation regarding aspects to highlight or the best way to discuss the passage with your friend.

These verses are not for the casual questioner but are rather for someone who is trying to "count the cost" of committing themselves to Jesus or who has already committed and needs to know how to live the Christian life. Most of these passages will bring about much soul-searching; all will help your friend to stare straight into the reality of living for Jesus.

Acts 2:42 and Romans 12 – Get Plugged in!

The new believers recorded in this passage became involved in the Christian community right away. They didn't live in seclusion away from fellow believers, rather they not only learned with, but ate, drank, and prayed with them as well. Any new believer from a Muslim background will need this kind of community. Community in the life of a believer is not only commanded (Hebrews 10:25) but is absolutely vital to the growth of each member.

Muslims are coming from a background in which their religion was also their way of life —there was no divorcing one from the other. Any Muslim who decides to follow Christ will need the fellowship they will no longer receive within their Muslim community. Getting them involved in church or a house Bible study (if they are not able to attend services) should be of highest priority. Help them to get plugged in to the true "umma" or "family" —that of the body of Christ. Study Romans 12 and I Corinthians 12 with them. Help them to gain a sense of the depth and strength of their new family —a place in the body of Christ. This will be of great encouragement to them.

Think Ahead: Though this may seem unconventional to our western way of thinking, if you disciple a new single believer, consider keeping on the look-out for a good husband/wife for them. Muslim families will want their children to marry Muslims (whether they are aware of the fact that their child is a Christian or not). If a suitable person can be presented by good friends first, their match-making plans could possibly be put on hold. Many will not object to a "religious" woman marrying their assumed-to-be Muslim son and most will at least consider a good man who asks for their assumed-to-be Muslim daughter's hand.

Relevant Rabbit Trail: Your friend decides to accept Jesus. You begin to disciple them and teach them what the Bible says about living for Jesus. Then one day, your friend asks you when they should tell their family. You know this could potentially cause them to be estranged, beaten, disowned, or all of the above. So what do you tell them? Read on for the Biblical perspective to this answer!

Acts 3:8-9 – Give God Glory

A man, lame for the entirety of his life, was given the gift of healing and new life in Christ. He lived in the midst of a Jewish nation. His family was Jewish. He even sat outside of the temple asking for alms due to his ailment. So when he was given physical and spiritual healing did he hide the fact? No, he "leaping up stood, and walked, and entered with them into the temple, walking, and leaping, and praising God. And all the people saw him walking and praising God." God is given glory, honor and praise in front of everyone who knew him.

When it comes to the question of telling family and friends about new found faith, there are many factors to consider and accordingly, every piece of advice must be drenched in prayer. On one hand, yes, they need to tell others. On the other hand, yes, they also need to be wise in the way they go about it. Some of the many factors to consider when giving advice include: Is their family devoted to Islam? Are they nominal Muslims? Is one member of their family or another more likely to be interested? Will they be in danger of physical harm? Deportation? Seclusion?

The above may seem extreme, but make no mistake, many Muslim families will not be pleased by the conversion of their son or daughter. Most will consider them apostates, infidels, and worthy of punishment. Depending on the type of family you are considering, there may need to be a gap of time before your friend is able to discuss their conversion with one or more members of their family.

My foremost piece of advice would be this —preach what you have practiced. Have your baby-believer friend start to share their testimony by simply living it before their family. Just as your own living testimony drew your friend to ask questions about God of you, so it will draw their families to ask about the difference they witness in their son or daughter. Then, as your friend is asked questions by their family or friends, they can answer in a gently, loving, and confident way.

Relevant Rabbit Trail: What about going to the mosque, praying five times a day, or practicing other inherently Islamic practices? This is a question that people like me stay awake at night praying over. As I proceed, let me first say this: going to the mosque, praying in a ritualistic posture, or fasting during a certain time of the year will not take a believer out of the Lord's hands.

In general, men and women both will gradually withdraw from mosque participation. Some choose to stop going cold-turkey, but most taper their activity a bit at a time. There are exceptions to this rule as well, as some choose to continue going in order to use it as a platform to discuss spiritual truths with their Muslim friends and bring Islam into question. This is a very person-by-person matter and, again, should be sought heavily through prayer.

Praying is a bit easier, as it is not necessarily the posture or time so much as the prayer itself that is the concern. They are no longer praying to "Allah" but to the Lord in Jesus' name. As long as that is the focus, whether they pray on their knees, prostrate on the floor, or with their head touching it, it doesn't really matter.

Finally, when it comes to fasting during the month of Ramadan, many choose to complete the fast. They are, however, doing it for a better reason. No longer do they fast in hopes to atone for their sins, but rather they fast and pray for the lost state of their families, friends, and homeland. You might even want to do it with them. Keep in mind that, as a follower of Jesus, we are told to fast and pray. Again, it doesn't matter so much as to the time or season of the fast, as much as the reason behind it.

Acts 4:19-20 – Right in the Sight of God

Make no mistake; the New Testament paints a very realistic look at the lives of believers, particularly new believers in hostile environments. The Acts of the Apostles are just that —acts— what they have done, where they have gone, what they have said, and how they have suffered. These verses are not coming from believers living cushy, persecution-free lives. Rather, they were under threat of persecution constantly. Paul, one of the main people in the book of Acts, is one of the most persecuted believers we know. Persecution is real and it may very possibly occur in the life of your new-believer friend. Verses like this will encourage and exhort them to do that which is right in the sight of God.

Acts 5:29, 40-42 and 30-32 – Obey God Rather than Men

Similarly to Acts 4:19-20, these verses encourage believers to do and say that which is right and true. Will it bring consequences? Yes. But that is the point.

Acts 8:26-40 and 14:19-27 – Explicit Obedience

Philip, a believer in Jesus Christ, lived entirely for his

Lord and Saviour. So when, one day, the Lord told him to go talk to a man he had never met and tell him about Jesus, Philip obeyed. Hearing the Lord speak through the Holy Spirit and direct us is incredible and something that must not be ignored. Communicate to your friend the fact that the Lord may, indeed, ask them to do things or say something that might not make sense right away —such as talking to a stranger, or their devout Muslim father about the Gospel.

Paul, commissioned of the Lord and sent to preach Jesus to the gentiles, suffered harsh persecution in the face of obedience. But still, he obeyed. He travelled from city to city, planting churches, preaching Jesus, and encouraging believers. Christ has called us to pick up our cross (Mark 8:4-35). He has also reminded us that if the world persecuted Him, we might as well accept, as fact, the notion of our own persecution (John 15:20). In verse 19 of our passage we are told that Paul was **stoned** for preaching the gospel and yet in verse 20, **the next day** he travelled to another city in order to preach there.

As a believer, we are called to follow the Lord with ready obedience. One day it might simply mean reading the Bible and loving Jesus. Another day it might mean sharing our beliefs with a friend, neighbor, or family member. It might be scary, but remind them that the Lord promises no one can take them out of His grasp (John 10:28).

Acts 19:18-20 – A New Man

When we are accepted into the family of God through Jesus Christ, we become new creatures (2 Corinthians 5:17). We are no longer ruled by sin or in bondage to the enemy. Any aspect of our "old man," therefore, that goes against Christ should be done away with, even if it is hard or costly. In this passage people, who beforehand practiced witchcraft, burned their books and implements which went with that practice. The net worth of these items came to a grand total of 50,000 pieces of silver! That's somewhere in the region of $32,000 to $37,000 US dollars! I'm pretty sure a monetary loss like that had to have hurt. But they did it anyway.

Important Side Note: I am not telling you to tell your new believer friend to burn the Qur'an; that would just be foolish. They should, however, stop reading it and treating it like gold. Other aspects of their previous faith to "do away with" would be prayer beads, treasured volumes of Muhammad's writings, and amulets such as the "evil eye."

Acts 20:24 – Ministry Received

"But none of these things move me...." When Paul said this, he was referencing a few verses previous where he stated that he knew "bonds and afflictions" were coming (vs. 23). Just like with your friend, persecution was a very present reality. That fact, however, did not stop Paul in the least from continuing to share the hope of the gospel with anyone who would listen.

Every single child of God is called to a different purpose and a different time, but all are called to share the gospel. Just as the new believers in Jerusalem were called to share it during a time of severe persecution (Matthew 28:18-20), so are we and your new-believer friend. That, ultimately, is the ministry which we have received —to testify the gospel of the grace of God.

Acts 28:30-31 – Preaching Still

Paul suffered through prison sentences, harsh treatment at the hands of his captors, and two years of a house-bound prison sentence. Through it all, he continued to preach the gospel with confidence. Though this may not be the calling for all of us, it is something to consider and keep in mind as we endeavor to tell those around us about the love and hope of Jesus Christ. Friends may turn away from us and family may disown us, but we still ought to preach the saving grace that has been given us.

Luke 10:39-42 – One Thing Needful

Depth, growth, and maturity in Christ come as a result of spending time with Him. Closeness to Christ is what will carry each person through trials and hardships, discouragement and persecutions. We are saved out of slavery and into a relationship with the Living God! Life may get busy, even serving the Lord through church participation or some other equally worthy activity may consume our days, but one thing is needful. We, along with Mary, need to be reminded to make spending time with our LORD the utmost priority on our list. This is of special importance for your new-believer friend. Our faith and understanding of both Jesus and the way we are to live will be grounded in the word of God. Spending time in the word is critical to the development of our spiritual growth.

I Cor. 3:6-17, 23 – The Increase

As your new believer friend begins to share the saving hope of Jesus with their friends or family, whether by word or deed, encourage them with this passage. They may not necessarily see their friend or family member accept Christ. As a matter of fact, they may encounter quite a bit of hostility to the very notion of doing such a thing. However, in God's great plan, every person and every testimony is used. Some plant seeds, some water them, some gather the increase. With many who are adamantly opposed to the gospel, it could potentially take a lot of planting and a lot of watering to produce that increase. Encourage your friend to not become discouraged when their testimony is not well received. Encourage them to continue living out their witness, knowing that Christ is completing a great work in them and in those they desire to reach.

I Cor. 15:58 – Labor Not in Vain

Though this verse is similar to those directly above, I think this is even more poignant. Your friend's life, their testimony, their witness, their prayer upon prayer upon prayer for their family and friends is not in vain.

Look at this verse closely. Firstly, believers are exhorted to be "steadfast, unmoveable, always abounding in the work of the Lord." Why is the Christian life to be so confidently lived? Because of "God, which giveth us the victory through our Lord Jesus Christ" (I Cor.15:57). Every believer has been given the victory over sin in Jesus Christ.

Jesus is the sole reason we live (Philippians 1:21), for in Him "we live, and move, and have our being" (Acts 17:28a). Through Jesus we are no longer bound to sin and Satan, but have an eternal relationship with the Lord on High. We are Christ's. We worship the Truth, live by it and share it because as we well know, "the truth shall set you free!" (John 8:32).

Secondly, we are told that our "labor is not in vain in the Lord." This should provide great amounts of encouragement. Our labor, our prayers, the many times we share the words of scripture, the many times we endeavor to live in a way that is pleasing unto the Lord, the opportunities presented to tell others about our testimony, will not occur in vain.

This is the second reason why we can confidently

live for the Lord. Our obedience to Christ's call on our lives, his commands to share the gospel, love those around us, and seek his face **will not** be in vain. The Lord will produce his great work in each of our lives and whether we see immediate results or not, we can live with the full confidence that "he which hath begun a good work in you will perform it until the day of Jesus Christ" (Philippians 1:6). Whether we are called to share the good news with someone because they are searching for God or simply because God desires to find in us obedience, it will not be done in vain. What a promise!

Chapter 10

Final Word

Congratulations! You've made it to the final chapter of this little book. I hope and pray that what has been written in these pages is both helpful and encouraging to you. It has been a blessing for me to write it, recounting the many ways God has taught me about these precious people. This chapter includes three remaining sections: scriptural principles not yet addressed, apologetics, and my final word on the whole book. Enjoy!

Scriptural Principles (not yet addressed)

Communion

If your friend is able to become a regular part of your church, there will undoubtedly come a point when they will encounter a communion service. As with any commanded act of service, it is important that they participate. Though your pastor will likely explain the meaning of communion, it would be beneficial for you to do so beforehand, as well.

There is nothing in communion that will be inherently difficult for a former Muslim to comprehend. Simply emphasize the following points:

1. Communion is a commanded act of **remembrance.**

Luke 22:19-20 clearly communicates this principle as does Matthew 2:26-28. It is important that your friend is clear on the fact that in no way does communion play a role in salvation of the individual. Communion is an act of remembrance, remembering what Jesus Christ did on the cross by giving His body and shedding His blood for the remission of our sins. Communion is an act of remembrance commanded by Jesus Himself. We are to regularly engage in it, reaffirming our faith in the atoning blood of Jesus Christ.

2. The grape juice and bread are **representative.**

This is an important principle that differs greatly from what former Muslims might have heard about the church. Though these rumors are not heard often, in some circles, Muslims believe that Christians actually drink blood. Due to the Catholic Church's belief of transubstantiation (believing that the communion bread and wine actually become the physical body and blood of Jesus) rumors have been around for a long time that Christians are cannibals. Emphasize the fact that when Jesus commanded his disciples to "do this in remembrance of me" He was quite obviously not eating Himself, nor do we believe anything of the sort. We eat and drink that which Christ did in his example —"wine" and bread.

3. Your church probably serves grape juice not "wine."

This is an important fact for your formerly Muslim friend. Let them know that the "wine" they will drink will undoubtedly be Welch's. If yours is one of the churches which serves both, please alert your friend as to which ring of cups is grape juice and provide the example by taking grape juice as well. Whatever your views on wine, for communion or otherwise, this will still be a difficult issue for your formerly Muslim friend. Avoid the issue and drink the grape juice. In all likelihood, that's what Jesus drank too!

Tithing

The action component of this principle is fairly contingent on whether your friend is able to regularly attend church. If they are, they will probably have questions about the practice of tithing. In many churches, it is a very public activity with buckets or other money-holding containers passed around. The Bible teaches at length on this principle. Your pastor will usually quote one or two verses in reference to tithing just before he offers up the prayer in order to receive it. Some churches won't say anything at all as the offering plate is passed around. I would encourage you to discuss the following three passages with your friend on this topic.

Tithing is an **act of worship**

I Chronicles 16:27-29 "Glory and honor are in his presence; strength and gladness are in his place. Give unto the LORD, ye kindreds of the people, give unto the LORD glory and strength. Give unto the LORD the glory due unto his name: bring an offering and come before him: worship the LORD in the beauty of holiness."

Tithing is one of the many ways through which we can glorify, honor, thank, and worship our LORD. He has given us everything we have, has supplied all of our needs, and tithing is a simple way of saying "thank you." It also says "I trust you for the future" when it is uncertain. Tithing can be difficult, especially for those in financial difficulties but, as we'll see below, God blesses all gifts and every giver.

Tithing is to be **regular and consistent.**

I Corinthians 16:1-2 "Now concerning the collection for the saints, as I have given order to the churches of Galatia, even so do ye. Upon the first day of the week let every one of you lay by him in store, as God hath prospered him, that there be no gatherings when I come."

The principle of weekly tithing is seen here. This, among other verses, is also where we get the principle of giving to the church. All throughout scripture, tithing is spoken of in direct relation to giving to God through His servants. In the Old Testament, sacrifices and tithes were given to God via members of the Levitical priesthood (Leviticus 27:30-33); in the New Testament they were given to the apostles and individual churches (Acts 11:29-30).

Tithing is to be **purposeful and potentially sacrificial.**

The Old Testament scripture in Leviticus 27:30-33 is where we get our traditional view of tithing 10% to the church. Since then, we have been given numerous New Testament portions of scripture to add to our understanding.

2 Corinthians 9:6-7 "But this I say, he which soweth sparingly shall reap also sparingly; and he which soweth bountifully shall reap also bountifully. Every man according as he purposeth in his heart, so let him give; not grudgingly, or of necessity: for God loveth a cheerful giver."

I Corinthians 16:1-2 speaks of giving out of our prosperity.

In Luke 22:1-4 Jesus points out a poor widow giving to the Lord out of her poverty. She was praised for giving "all she had."

Clearly, tithing is to reflect both giving out of prosperity and poverty. It is to be an act of worship and gratitude, and one which might very well be sacrificial.

Baptism

Baptism is one of those "tread-cautiously" subjects when speaking with former Muslims or those of dominant anti-Christian religious backgrounds. To many families, baptism is the final nail that seals the proverbial coffin. Even if a son or daughter reveals the fact that they rejected Islam in order to follow Jesus, the family will feel that some hope remains. When, however, they get baptized, some families will officially disown their "wayward" children. Husbands have divorced wives, wives have left husbands to live with their parents, sons and daughters have been disowned, and members of families have been shunned over this one act.

In our western mind-set, we think of baptism as an exciting event in the life of a believer. Baptism usually occurs in a church surrounded by numerous family members and friends as well as church members to witness the occasion. It might even happen at a member's house where there is a pool for the occasion and a barbeque lunch afterward. Regardless of the location, it is a joyous event, declaring one's faith in Jesus Christ.

For much of the non-western world, however, baptism is much more than proclaiming to those who love and support them that they are following the same Lord. Baptism means that they are literally rejecting everything they have ever known. It not only represents dying to self and living to the Lord, but dying to family, friends, position, status, wealth, love, and community.

Baptism is a very important step in the life of any believer and is definitely something that should be encouraged but it should not be pushed. The subject can be introduced and often times, as with the Ethiopian eunuch (Acts 8:35-38), will be voluntarily desired by the new believer. When desire to get baptized is expressed by your friend, go through what baptism is (Acts 8:13, 9:18, 19:5; Romans 6:3-4; Galatians 3:27), help them think through what baptism will mean to both them and their families, and then help them organize the event (meeting with the pastor beforehand, setting a date at the church, etc). Be ready to be the shoulder your friend might need to cry on after the event. Depending on the type of family, repercussions could be very mild to quite severe.

Apologetics

Apologetics, put simply, is the defense of what you believe. It is taking a question or an accusation about your beliefs and effectively giving an answer, "to every man that asketh you a reason of the hope that is in you." 1 Peter 3:15. Below you will find three "hot" topics that most Muslims will want to discuss. Read on and be prepared to "give a reason"!

The Trinity

When the subject of the trinity is brought up, Muslims are often convinced that Christians worship three separate gods —the father, the son and the spirit. They have likely been taught this from the time they were in diapers. If your Muslim friend should believe that you, too, worship three separate deities, here's what you do.

1. Adamantly deny it. Muslims can be quite fervent in their religious beliefs and even nominal Muslims will stand up for what they think is true or against what they view as blasphemy. Their saying that you worship three gods is paramount to blasphemy —act accordingly. Show some religious fervor. It's a good thing!

2. Point them to scripture. The trinity is difficult to explain to Christians, let alone those who believe something so different from you and me. Explain the trinity as best you can, but reaffirm the fact that we absolutely **do not** believe in three gods. The verses below will help point your friend to the fact that all throughout the Holy Scriptures, God is referenced as One. Jesus even got in trouble because He said He and the Father (God) were one. He never claimed to not be God —or a different god.

Deuteronomy 6:4, "Hear, O Israel: The LORD our God is one LORD."

John 10:30, "I and my Father are one."

Romans 3:30, "Seeing it is one God, which shall justify the circumcision by faith, and uncircumcision through faith."

I Corinthians 8:4, "…there is none other God but one."

I Corinthians 8:6, "But to us there is but one God, the Father, of whom are all things, and we in him; and one Lord Jesus Christ, by whom are all things, and we by him."

• Make note of the fact that this verse speaks of God and Jesus in the exact same terms, equating one with the other.

The beauty of the trinity is this: ONE God is revealed in different ways. The trinity is the word we use in describing the various ways in which God has revealed Himself – as Father, as Son, and as Spirit (more on the Spirit below).

The Sonship of Jesus

This is a "sticking point" for a lot of Muslims. When they hear "Son of God" they think you are saying ***God had sexual relations with a woman and pro-duced a son.*** Nothing could be farther from the truth! Again, this is blasphemy —act accordingly!

Jesus' "sonship" in the Bible serves to equate Him

with God. Just as a person who is known as a "son of the desert" is someone who epitomizes living in that part of the land, so Jesus as the "son of God" epitomizes God. He represents and fully reveals God (Hebrews 1:1-3).

In John 1:1 Jesus is described as the Word of God. He is also called the Way, the Truth, the Bread of Life, the Light of the World, and the Door of Salvation (John 14:6, 6:35, 8:12, and 10:9 respectively). He is no more the product of God and a goddess or a human being than He is a literal piece of wheat bread, a 100 Watt light bulb, or an oak panel through which we enter a building. The sonship of Jesus is one of God's ways of expressing, explaining, representing, and revealing the ONE God we worship.

The Holy Spirit

Though this is a lesser known argument than the previous two, many Muslims believe that the Comforter that Jesus speaks of is not the Holy Spirit, but the prophet Muhammad. There are a few verses which will quickly point out to your Muslim friend that the Comforter could, in no way, be Muhammad.

The Holy Spirit will **testify of Jesus.**

John 15:26, "But when the Comforter is come, whom I will send unto you from the Father, even the Spirit of truth, which proceedeth from the Father, he shall testify of me."

John 14:26, "But the Comforter, which is the Holy ghost, whom the Father will send in my name, he shall teach you all things, and bring all things to your remembrance, whatsoever I have said unto you."

The Holy Spirit was to **first appear during a specific time.**

John 16:7, "Nevertheless I tell you the truth; It is expedient for you that I go away: for if I go not away, the Comforter will not come unto you; but if I depart, I will send him unto you."

Acts 1:4-8, "And, being assembled together with [the disciples], commanded them that they should not depart from Jerusalem, but wait for the promise of the Father, which, saith [Jesus] ye have heard of me. For John truly baptized with water; but ye shall be baptized with the Holy Ghost not many days hence. When they therefore were come together, they asked of him, saying, Lord, wilt thou at this time restore again the kingdom to Israel? And he said unto them, It is not for you to know the times or the seasons, which the Father hath put in his own power. But ye shall receive power, after that the Holy Ghost is come upon you: and ye shall be witnesses unto me both in Jerusalem, and in all Judaea, and in Samaria, and unto the uttermost part of the earth."

The Holy Spirit **has a specific job.**

John 16:8-11, "And when he is come, he will reprove

the world of sin, and of righteousness, and of judgment: of sin, because they believe not on me; of righteousness, because I go to my Father, and ye see me no more; of judgment, because the prince of this world is judged."

Final Word

If I had to give you one piece of advice regarding everything in this book, one tidbit to get you started down the road of relationship witnessing, one "tool" to put in your witnessing belt, it would be this: ASK QUESTIONS. There is perhaps nothing more powerful than this simple exercise. I hope you've seen how vital question asking can be (chapter 3). All your friend may need is one question mark at the end of a sentence to begin their personal journey to the One, True God and the Salvation He offers.

One Last Story

Muslims believe that Allah counts their prayers. When they die, those prayers will be tallied and put into the pile of "good" things they have done. Hopefully their good will outweigh their bad. If they've been to Mecca, then one prayer they prayed there counts for one-hundred thousand prayers offered up elsewhere.

When I learned of this useful information I asked my friend three simple questions to start her walking down the path toward Truth. Our two-minute, whispered-inside-a-mosque conversation went like this:

Me: Who's counting your prayers?

Her: God

Me: How many prayers do you have to pray to be holy enough for him?

Her: *silence*

Me: Can you ever pray enough to earn holiness before a perfectly holy God?

Her: ... No.

Pray and ask questions! Pray —and **question**— your Muslim friends to the Truth. Pray and question them to Salvation! Pray and question them into eternity.